DEAR GOD!
WHAT'S HAPPENING TO US?

Other Books by Lynn Grabhorn

Excuse Me, Your Life Is Waiting

The Excuse Me, Your Life Is Waiting *Playbook*

Beyond the Twelve Steps

lynn grabhorn

DEAR GOD! WHAT'S HAPPENING TO US?

Halting Eons of Manipulation

HAMPTON ROADS
PUBLISHING COMPANY, INC.

for the evolving human spirit

Cover design by Steve Amarillo
Cover photograph copyright © 1997, Comstock, Inc.
www.comstock.com

Hampton Roads Publishing Company, Inc.
1125 Stoney Ridge Road
Charlottesville, VA 22902

434-296-2772
fax: 434-296-5096
e-mail: hrpc@hrpub.com
www.hrpub.com

If you are unable to order this book from your local
bookseller, you may order directly from the publisher.
Call 1-800-766-8009, toll-free.

           Library of Congress Cataloging-in-Publication
Data

Grabhorn, Lynn.
  Dear God, what's happening to us? / Lynn Grabhorn.
      p. cm.
  ISBN 1-57174-384-7 (alk. paper)
  1. Spiritual life--Miscellanea. I. Title.
  BF1999 .G677 2003
  158.1--dc21

    2002154469

10 9 8 7 6 5 4 3 2 1

Printed on acid-free paper in Canada

table
of
contents

introduction

Please! Read this first
before you begin chapter one.

If you flip through the pages of this book before really getting into it, your hair will probably stand on end because the information may look forbidding, to say the least. It is not.

This book is about how exceptional and indispensable you are to the human race, and to all of existence.

If the early pages of this book seem to impart a tone that is more down than up, please know that is not the case. No longer!

This book is about freedom: unimaginable personal freedom that has never been experienced before on this planet, or in the history of mankind, or in the history of you as a human, or in the history of the Isness.

Dear God! What's Happening to Us?

If the book scares you a bit at first, that's probably all right if the end result will be to engage you in the simple steps to bring you this unprecedented liberty. Just know this:

The information in this book has never been released before!

While I'm not so sure I care to enjoy the distinction of being the one to do just that . . . well . . . here I am.

The information in this book is shocking. And it is true. But above all, it is easily surmountable.

The information in this book could be called "scare tactics." Granted, those who say that may be right, for my objective has surely been to get your attention and then push you with ease to a new level of existence that has never been known to any human, ever before.

The truth is, we've been had. We've been used. We've been hoodwinked, but . . . *BUT!!!!!!* . . . all for the sake of the incomprehensible dawning that's coming down the pike.

So please, just stay with me to the end of the book and find out how easy it will be to change what has been imprisoning us all, for so very long.

Actually, this book is about our participation— willingly though unconsciously at the moment—in a scheme so well concealed and so formidable that it boggles the mind. And yet, this scheme that we agreed to participate in was so filled with love for the creation of Life known as human, so filled with love for *all* of Life, and so filled with love and compassion and caring for all of existence, that we were willing to sacrifice countless lifetimes of struggle and discord just to bring it all to the eventual end that you knew would one day come about— *IF* we persevered. Meaning, of course, the ultimate payoff that is not long away.

That incredible day is very close at hand. But *your* freedom can be immediate.

So please! Read without fear. Read without alarm, knowing that truth is often unpleasant. If you fall into the disbelief of what we have all been caught up in and agreed to, allow your fears and outrage surface. *But know that there is a way out.* Not in some nebulous tomorrow as so many self-help books offer, but now.

Please! Read on in anticipation, not fear. What is imparted early on in these pages is only necessary to lay the foundation for you to spring to a newness never before extended to the human being. That is a truth. Remember:

The information in this book has
never been allowed to be released before.

So go with it. Find out how to strike back at what has been imprisoning you and all of us, and make a difference, not only to you, but to all of mankind.

The steps presented here are so absurdly simple. Yet they are crucial if you desire the freedom that is being offered. If that sparks a curiosity within you, then read on, and make it happen.

My love and my thanks to you,
Lynn Grabhorn

(PS:) Reference to "The Others" is capitalized only for ease of reading, not out of respect for the species.

chapter one

what's coming down

How are you feeling these days? How's your life going? How about your moods? Or your partner's moods, or your friends' or your dog's, or your coworkers'? Is everybody a little nuts?

On the other hand, if you're feeling great and are without stress, strain, or struggle, and have a life that's flowing with ease, and your partner and kids do too, then Wow! More power to you. Ninety-nine percent of the folks on this planet would call you weird! Feeling good is not the norm now, and for most people, it never will be again.

This is a book about Light and dark, and you and me and several billion other folks. It's a book that has within its pages some rather mind-boggling information that's never been allowed to be released before. Because of that, it's going to take a few chapters of fairly wild background

1

before we get to the heart of what we can so easily do to remove—for our individual selves at least—this formidable clamp of control by entities of the dark with which we have so unconsciously been living, for so very long.

So, is this really a self-help book? Well, sort of, kind of, maybe, but not exactly!

It's hardly big news that our world is in a scary mess. Oh sure, we've been through bad times before in our history and come out of them: Dark Ages, the plagues, the Crusades, and so on. But the ugly times we went through then never had the hard-hitting blow-by-blow media coverage we have today which so readily fuels the fires of our own personal anxieties.

First, of course, there's the rest of the world, and then there's us: you and me. Granted, we may not be entangled in things like wide-spread starvation, or women beatings, or mutilations by terrorists, but in truth, how are the lives of most of us running right now? Smoothly? Serenely? Happily?

Not to belabor the point, but let's face it, back in the Dark Ages, folks were not confronted with global warming, or world-wide terrorism, or rampant chronic fatigue syndrome, or the breaking down of religious structures, or kids who were diagnosed with everything from dyslexia to ADD.

In today's society, it seems that anxiety is the only thing that keeps us going. It's what feeds us. "Stress" has become the norm for just about every living soul on this planet, whether it's because of so many wars, or job security, or the stock market, or local atrocities, or religion. We've become a species of nail-biting, uptight human beings who have a damnably hard time finding anything but fleeting moments of happiness in our lives.

So now comes the twenty-four-billion-dollar question: "Why?" Why is all of this disunity and dysfunction happening to the vast majority of us? Why are we, in every corner and every nook and cranny of this world, all so terribly troubled and uneasy? Why? Why? Why?

Who's Gonna Believe?

This is a book about a few simple things we can do just once—to drastically change and safeguard our lives. Unfortunately, those few simple things will have to wait to unfold until close to the end of the book, because if I put them right up front, you would absolutely know, beyond any shadow of a doubt, that I had flipped out, lost it, cracked up, or become psychotic.

This is a book about the so-called Light and dark of our universe, and what we can do to distance ourselves from the influence of the latter, which is far more powerful in our lives than any of us have ever realized. In truth, I had to think long and hard about writing this book for that very reason, for I'm not too fond of the likelihood of being called an eccentric kook.

With my last book on many best-seller lists (*Excuse Me, Your Life Is Waiting*) and still selling well, everything in me said, "Don't write this, you blockhead, or *Excuse Me . . .* will become obsolete faster than you could say, 'Oh dear me, I goofed!'"

Nonetheless, though I am anything but a courageous, crusading kind of person, I knew the truth had to be written, for it is the truth as I know it to be, and truth as I have seen it in action.

Granted, there may be precious few who will believe what they find in these pages, calling what they read nothing but a frivolous collection of fairy tales. But for those precious few who take this to heart, not only will *their* lives change dramatically for the better (that would be putting it mildly), they will make a significant difference to this planet.

If you are one of those precious few, then blessings unto you a million fold. You're in for one fantastic ride!

The Last Stand

It goes without saying that a book needs to have a healthy number of pages in order for a publisher to charge a price that will, after everyone takes their cut, still make him a decent profit. But I decided not to "pad" the information I want to impart. Small in page numbers or not, this book will be made of pure meat, not fill. And so with that in mind, let's get down to it for the first "Holy Cow, are you really serious????" (Or else, "That does it lady; that's as far as I'm reading!")

Most religions on our earth have alluded for centuries to the "war in the heavens" between Light and dark. In actuality, that's what the so-called "Dark Ages" were all about, and the plagues, and the Crusades, and that's what we're all into now, from rain forests to chronic fatigue syndrome.

But now our so-called troubled times are huge. Now, we either pull ourselves out of the mess we've all allowed to happen once again, or this time around, mankind can kiss itself goodbye. This is the last stand, and time is of the essence.

The truth of this long-lived war is that at the moment, we're fighting a losing battle. Those who are not of the Light are winning this round, thanks to all of the clever manipulations to which most of us have turned deaf ears, blind eyes, and indifferent senses.

In pages to come, I'm going to relay what has been told me as to why, when, and how this war in the ethers started in the first place, why it has reignited so aggressively now, how you personally have been caught up in it, what you can do about it, and what the outcome is going to be IF enough of us will engage in the simple steps needed to bring this horrible manipulation to a halt, at least for our own lives.

Outlandish?

How many self-help books have you bought lately? And how many have you wanted to toss out before getting very far, or at least wished the author had given you some more clearly defined silver bullets?

The fact is that no matter what self-help book you've picked up (and perhaps put in a paper bag so no one would know), not one of them can possibly give you a silver bullet without some very unusual personal housecleaning, which are the simple steps we'll be discussing. All I'm saying is that as off-the-wall as this book may seem to you, it's important. It's really important!

I've just come through what I'm writing about, and have friends who have been through it who are now starting to live different lives. Their funds are beginning to increase, most of their despair is gone, along with their anxiety or even boredom. For some, relationships have even shaped up. But perhaps most important of all, their bizarre physical discomforts are gone, and that unknown, elusive little thing called "joy" is starting to wave them in the face for the first time in a long, long time, or ever.

A few simple quiet procedures, that's all this book is about. You can do them in bed or in your car, with your friends or on the bus, with your spouse or by yourself, with candles glowing and incense burning or walking on the beach in quiet, contemplative moments. All that's called for are some meaningful moments where you can "go inside," find that special place that is You, and then, one by one, call these simple steps into play. That's all. That's truly all! With them, you change your life. With them, you change the direction of this world.

Yes, you could turn to the back of this book right now to find out what these steps are. If you want to do that, go ahead. But do NOT . . . repeat . . . do NOT attempt to do them until you've read everything that is so important for you to know first. I'm serious. You need the background before diving in, or the simple steps that are being offered will be about as effective as trying to climb Mt. Everest on skis. They'll accomplish nothing.

So if you must peek, go ahead, but then come on back and fill in the background that is vital.

"Shitsville" Yet?

On a scale of one to ten, with ten being disgustingly happy and one being ready to take the permanent sleeping pills, where are you?

Maybe you're one of those relatively rare creatures

who's fairly content, but with a pesky little itch of some sort. Perhaps that itch is your job, or your house, or funds (granted, that may not be such a small itch), or even your partner. At any rate, something's not working the way you'd like it to, and it's been going on for longer than you think is reasonable. So where are you on the scale? Like maybe a five? Or even a six?

Or maybe you really are one of those unheard of souls who are, in honest-to-God truth, full of vim and vigor, bursting with enthusiasm, alive with passion, and in love with life. Like a nine pushing ten. Even if that is so (and I do so heartily congratulate you if it is), please don't throw this book out. These steps are for everybody, whether at zero and about to gobble down some cyanide, or at nine to ten and positively drooling in wellbeing.

Most of us would probably fall in somewhere around the five to six category, which would be, "I'm makin' it, but not enjoying it that much, and damn, it all seems so bloody hard! Not to mention I don't feel so hot."

Even if you used to be a cushy six or seven, maybe you've more recently found yourself tumbling slowly down to the rocky fours or below where life has taken a somewhat frightening, unexplainable turn toward "Shitsville." It's as if you've been slowly and unknowingly covered with this unseen veil of distress, and a new and different "you" has turned from what used to be an upbeat seven, to a somber four-minus. "What in heaven's name has happened to me? What's going on here? I never used to be like this, or feel like this!"

Then again, maybe what we're talking about hasn't hit you yet. But if it has, how bad has it gotten for you physically or emotionally? Are you dragging your rear, feeling short-tempered, exhausted, tearful, pessimistic, defeated, or plain old fed up?

Or have you already advanced to the unnumbered stage of shortness of breath and heavy breathing, or torturous headaches, or sleepless nights accompanied with heavy sweats, or a body that feels like it's made of lead, or sensations of your insides being fried to the quick like the Colonel's chicken? And yes, there's more, but we don't have to be that grim—yet.

The good news is that if what you're experiencing is being induced by the unseen, you can bring it to a halt rather quickly. Perhaps even more importantly, if none of this has started with you yet, you'll be able to ward it off completely. I did not ward off this unpleasantness because I didn't know it was coming. But you can. I promise you, you can.

Major, Major, *Major* Disclaimer

Surely you've heard of chronic fatigue syndrome (CFS), and along with that you've probably heard of that other thing called fibromyalgia. They're often referred to in tandem. If you're dragging around, you could be one who has contracted one of these diseases.

And surely you've heard of the various types of diabetes, and how rampant this disease is in our culture today. If you have rapidly swinging moods along with rapidly changing physical ups and downs, you very possibly may have a type of diabetes.

My point is, if you're not feeling well physically, *get yourself checked*, preferably with more than one doctor.

If you're severely depressed, get yourself checked and remain open to the doctors' opinions or recommendations. Everyone knows we're living on antidepressants these days. (Didn't you ever wonder why?)

Many doctors don't know a great deal about CFS, or that it is, indeed, a virus. If you believe, after checking out the CFS symptoms on the Internet or at the library, that you may have this disease, for heaven's sake find someone who will treat it, for it is widely believed to be treatable.

How-ev-er!!! Once you have been thoroughly checked and find you don't have diabetes but are still having huge mood and body swings, or have been checked and find that whatever your doctor is giving you for CFS or fibromyalgia isn't working, or that your antidepressants aren't doing what you'd hoped they would do, or that your blood pressure is fine, and your heart, and your thyroid, etc. have no problems, then know that there is still another avenue for you to follow. This is the avenue of the Changing of the Guard, the secret weapon for all of us who are embodied as humans. All of us. Everybody!

But take care, here. If you've already jumped out of the plane without a parachute on and have a crippling disease, these steps are still important and may make your life more manageable, *but they are in no way a guarantee to cure you.*

If you've lived a life of doubt and worry and fear, ending up with an illness that has been diagnosed as incurable, these steps are still important and may help to change the worrisome feelings that flow from you, *but they are in no way a guarantee to cure you.*

These steps, alone, will not cure illness, nor will they plunk into your hands the winning Super Lotto ticket. They won't cure your diabetes, or your cancer, or whatever else you may have, for only careful attention to your doctor and your attitude may do that. And, they most surely won't change a crappy marriage into the Prince and Cinderella.

What these steps will do is:

1. halt any further lowering of that unseen veil of chronic physical or emotional suffering that so many of us in this world are now experiencing, and/or

2. prevent the physical and emotional horrors altogether, and

3. allow you a life you've probably never thought possible.

So please! Don't call me, e-mail me, or write me (or the publisher) with your specific problems, illnesses, or symptoms. I'm not a doctor, and I'm not a counselor, and I will flat-out not answer such questions. I'm someone who has been through the gates of physical, spiritual, emotional, and mental hell in the past few years, as so many are going through now or are about to go through, and I've come out on the other side because I finally found out how to get the torture stopped.

This is a dual-pronged do-it-yourself process. It's for those who might like to have a little bit of insurance against what otherwise may be just around the corner. And it's a do-it-yourself program for those who have already dropped down into a three or below, where symptoms are unexplainable, and mysterious aches and pains are coming from nowhere, and where doctors are able to offer no answers.

It is my sincere hope that no matter how good or bad your life may be at this moment, you'll find the desire to involve yourself with this simple process. All I ask is that you get checked out first, however you choose. Then, whether you find you're in the pink of health or not, see if the few minutes required to do these steps aren't worth warding off a potential disaster of hugely unhappy proportions. You'll have nothing to lose, and everything imaginable to gain.

Who Qualifies

If you've ever taken a writing class, you were told to weave your story around the Big Five *W*s, the Who, What, Where, When, and Whys of the event you're writing about, particularly if your story is for a newspaper.

Well, the What, When, Where, and Whys of our story are fairly complex, but the Who of those that are being affected—or may be affected—with this baffling, debilitating phenomenon that people are going through or will be going through, and that are emanating from the wars in the heavens, is fairly simple.

Everyone qualifies. Whether metaphysical or born-again, agnostic or spiritual, a "never-gave-it-much-thought" person, or deeply devoted to your religion, you're at risk.

If you've been on any sort of a spiritual path for the

last ten years or so, meaning anything from going to channeled sessions to doing the channeling yourself, or reading tarot cards, or calling the psychic hotline, you qualify.

If you've never thought much about religion or spirituality, but have at times wondered where you came from, or why you're here, or what your purpose is, or what force made all of this, or how the stars got there in the first place, you qualify.

If you're breathing, you qualify!

The Big Prize: Us!

The war between Light and dark in the heavens is as old as this universe. And by "universe," I mean everything we can see and not see in all dimensions, all realities, and, if you want to get really far out, in all time frames, past, present, or future.

Once the human started to evolve, it became clear to those who were watching that something very special was starting to happen with this species that had never been seen in the universe before.

The human being, in its third dimension, was fast becoming a highly desirous and heavily sought after creature, for, unlike anything that had ever been seen before, all of the secrets of Life, all of the secrets of beingness (if there is such a word), and all of the secrets of existence were present within each and every body. Damn fine prize for those who were treasure seekers.

And so, for reasons we'll soon see, "The Others," meaning those not of 100 percent pure Light, decided this was something they wanted for themselves, and have been working toward that goal for eons. Which means that we—the human race—are where the action has been for a long time within this universe. And it's been the seeking of this prize that has brought about so many ages of despair in our world, as well as the one we're going through now.

This time around, though, we've got a comeback. This time around we have in preparation an event of such unprecedented proportions that we'll be able to say, "No more manipulation, you guys: We've had it." Granted, to get to that place will take a bit of doing on our parts, but only a little, and then the worst of the travails of humanity will soon be a thing of the past for those of us who desire to join in the fun.

But "big event" notwithstanding, this intensified bounty hunting could affect every one of us on the planet. A frightening thought? Yes, it could be, *but it need not be!*

Why Take a Chance?

All of us, bar none, are being directly and adversely impacted by "The Others" right now. Every single one of us, and we have been for eons past in our history.

15

Dear God! What's Happening to Us?

However, not all of us will be targets for what they're doing to humanity these days. Maybe you'll be a target, maybe not. Maybe your spouse, or one of your employees, or maybe the Base Commander. These treasure hunters are after physical things we humans can offer them that they don't have, and can not find anywhere else. So who's to know which of us has what they want?

And please, I'm not necessarily talking about alien abductions here, although that's a small part of their treasure hunts. I'm talking about these unseen beings using us for exotic reasons that will cause us to feel thoroughly miserable, both physically and emotionally.

But whether or not they decide to use any one of us, as they did me, we are all directly and constantly under their daily influence. Either way, why take a chance on it starting, or continuing?

This is not a matter of who may be perceived to be a better or worse person, or more emotionally stable than another, or richer, or better educated. While not everyone will be in for the painful physical ride I have just come out of as a result of these dark guys tampering with my body, all but about one percent of our population has been affected directly in their personal lives by them since (and before) the day they were born.

Some who are the most likely to be severely affected by these beings, such as myself, actually signed up for this madness (not in our conscious awareness) by being duped

16

into it. But now that the wars are heating to a fever pitch, anyone could be marked for use, simply because of their appealing genetic structure.

All right, then, what do we have so far?

1. We Are All Being Affected

These dark entities, who have come originally from outside this universe, are currently affecting or completely controlling billions of human lives, and have been since humans came into existence, though now more severely than ever.

2. Many Will Be More Severely Affected

Because of the urgency of the times, The Others will be targeting a sizable group of humans to use for their own selfish reasons. This involves thoroughly unpleasant physical horrors that I would not wish on my worst enemy, if I had one. It is not fun, it is horrific, and if I were being offered this chance to ward off what I went through, I would jump at it.

Our Contracts and Good Intentions

You may be one who signed up for something that would, in some manner, help mankind. Now granted, what you think of mankind at this moment may be less than desirable to speak out loud. Nonetheless, before you came into this third-dimensional reality on this magnificent planet, you may have signed a contract to do something—maybe big, maybe small—in behalf of mankind, simply because you have always loved this human existence.

You knew before coming in that our species was in critical trouble, so you signed up with some who were legitimate lovers of the Light, and, in your eagerness, some who were not.

Maybe your signing a contract was to help a certain group wake up. Maybe it was just to help one person. Or maybe . . . and here's the biggie . . . it was to help mankind become, eventually, more than he is now, more than petty grievances and gripes, more than abusive actions, more than wars and atrocities, more than lack and emotional pain. Whatever it was you wanted to do before coming back in here, if you signed on, it was because you wanted to help. It's just that you may have been deceived into signing up with "The Others."

Actually, every one of us has made all manner of contracts before coming in here. But those "normal" kind of contracts are not what I'm talking about. The one so many of us made with The Others was not normal, and you may have been a bit hasty in your eagerness to sign on. God knows, I was.

You don't have to be a rabbi, or a guru, or a humanitarian to have signed this thing. You could be a jockey, a housewife, a major CEO, or a ski bum. It doesn't matter. If you signed this rather unusual contract, you did it because something in you, somewhere, wanted to help this endangered species called "human" that you have either consciously or unconsciously come to love.

When you read the beautiful story of creation and the story of what is soon to be offered to our entire universe, you'll understand why "The Others" are to be pitied, as well as feared.

For reasons that are frankly sad, they need not only what this universe has—which they have never had—but most especially now, what we as humans have. To accomplish this, they have become our guides, our consciousness, and even our "higher selves," for they know that without discovering and being able to use this special treasure that can come only from entities living in this universe of Light, they will exist in near nothingness, and never in Life.

What they seek is immortality. What they are coming to realize is that they can never have it unless a way is found to uncover the secret of this universe, held so amazingly in the human body.

And so, this large group of darks devised a plan long ago to attempt to maintain their existence. There was nothing malicious or villainous in their intent, only the need for survival. When time began to run out for them to successfully reap the necessary rewards from their treasure hunts, they devised a plan to covertly sell as many humans as possible on how to help humanity, and in the process, hopefully help themselves, The Others.

Some of us signed up simply to have our frequencies raised to push mankind's wake-up process.

Some of us signed up to allow microscopic parts of our brains to be removed to create living tissue for memory chips to be used in computers outside of this universe.

Some of us signed up to have samples of our DNA removed to be placed in new types of experimental bodies being created in the unseen.

Some of us signed up to have microscopic portions of our hearing mechanisms removed in order to allow experimentation with unexplored forms of hearing.

Some of us signed up to have infinitesimal pieces of our eye units removed for the same reasons, and various glands, and various organs.

Some, including me, signed up to have entire new bodies created directly from our own, in a higher dimension, simply to see if it could be done. For if it could be accomplished from our third/fourth dimension to fifth/sixth dimension, then (as I was told) it could be done at the next level, and the next, until the being known as human would ultimately be able to live in higher dimensions never before deemed to be possible for mass, meaning us. The fallacy in that theory was, of course, that no cloned entity, regardless of frequency, can ever carry the spark of Life we call a Soul. But most of us didn't think of that, at the time.

Science fiction? No. Just an uncaring group of beings in the unseen who may have had the best of intentions for themselves, but who could have cared less about the deleterious effects these experiments would impart upon the human body, not to mention the human psyche.

Nonetheless, just as we had agreed to have these entities of the dark guide us in lifetime after lifetime, we also agreed to allow them to use us for what we thought would be in the best interest of mankind. Could we really have been that stupid? Well, yes, under the circumstances, we could have, and we were.

But we have an out. Though cosmic law says that a contract is a contract and quite unbreakable until, and unless, the circumstances under which that contract was made should change, the circumstances have now changed. And that, by God, is our out, with or without that stupid contract!

chapter two

the first
three years

The gal in the wings of the meeting hall was having a hard time adjusting my portable microphone. For some reason, she couldn't get it clipped to my shirt and couldn't seem to get the button in my back pants pocket undone so she could slip the battery pack into it. I was about as "up" physically as I could manage, but every second of standing around while she fiddled was pulling me down energetically.

God only knows how I ever made it to that speaking engagement. If it hadn't been for a dear friend who agreed to go with me, hold me up, push me when needed, and "mother" me on and off the plane to our suite and onto the stage, I would not have made it. But now, with all of this fiddling, I was getting scared. Too much more fussing with this damn mike, and I'd have to cancel out.

Dear God! What's Happening to Us?

I heard the introduction being made, a long-winded thing about how I had arrived at this lofty point in life, then finally my name was announced. I had gone through this speaking routine many times since my book had become so popular, and usually I loved it. But at this moment, I wasn't sure I could even make it onto the stage.

The applause began . . . I commanded a head-high walk out to greet the hundreds of folks who were, by then, on their feet and cheering as well as applauding. I forced a huge smile and grandiose wave as I said to myself over and over, "Do it! You can do this. Just do it!" I would get through this for these wonderful people. Somehow, someway, I would get through this.

And I did, but just barely. When we got back to the hotel room, I collapsed like a wet dish rag, did my best to make conversation with my friend, and finally folded into the horror that I knew was waiting for me in bed. The "energies" had let up just enough to allow me to speak. Now, back in the hotel room, it would be back to business as usual, the grisly new energies that had somehow overtaken me recently. I dreaded the night.

The first three years of physical discomfort that had been somewhat bearable had become a thing of the past. What was happening to me now was indescribable, and excruciating. Yes, I had somehow made it to this speaking engagement, but I knew that it would be my last unless there was a drastic change in whatever it was that was going on with me.

Sleep in the hotel room that night would not come. What had changed from the last three years? What were these new, ghastly energies? Why were they increasing? How much longer? Why was it happening? Who was trying to hurt me? Was I to exist like this forever? Oh dear God in heaven, *can't anyone help me?*"

"Excuse Me, Your Life Is Waiting"

I was not one who started on the elusive path of spiritual awakening early in life. In fact, I was in my mid-fifties before stumbling onto one of those forks in the road that comes up for us now and then throughout life—the fork that says, "No, no, not down that path. You've already been there/done that. Here's a new direction. Take it!" And I did, with a gusto that was new, even to me.

Up until then, I had been everything from a go-fer in New York City for a large photography studio, to various spots in advertising, to the founder of a well-respected national audio-visual company in Hollywood. How I ever ended up going from the world of advertising sales and audio-visuals to running my own mortgage brokerage companies for almost two decades is still a mystery to me, but I did, and for the most part, enjoyed it.

Somewhere in the middle of those two decades it dawned on me that I should be making a lot more money than I was, a fact that was a persistent annoyance to me, or more like a sharp thorn in my side. I mean, here I'd been on this lofty spiritual journey for almost ten years, and was still having a hard time paying my bills. It was depressing.

Ah, but then one wonderful day, some new insightful material came my way, and I realized in an instant that something was about to change. I also knew that this material was so important, I'd be writing a book about it.

Within days I started my research for the book, mostly on weekends, of course, as I still had my little mortgage brokerage to run. And sure enough, the more work and research I put into the book, the more I noticed nice little financial changes happening, along with some truly innovative ideas to greatly increase my income.

The turn-around wasn't overnight, but within eighteen months of living every day with the principles I was writing about on weekends, my income had grown to almost the highest tax deduction in the IRS books.

I was having a ball with my mortgage business that had now grown to a state-wide organization, and I was having a ball writing. Except for some strange and very uncommon mood swings that seemed to coincide with occasional periods of extreme fatigue, I was thoroughly enjoying my life, my income, my weekend writing, and giving precious little thought to what was happening to me physically or emotionally.

Once the book was finished, it wasn't long before a major publisher asked to sign on. *Excuse Me, Your Life Is Waiting* broke out of the starting gate running full speed ahead, and it seemed to me that the universe had outdone itself in rewarding me with the verification of what I had written about. *Excuse Me . . .* was fast becoming a best seller, and I was in heaven. Almost.

The first year after the book's release, I traveled from one end of the country to the other, giving seminars and speaking. I did think it a bit strange that in Key West I was battling severe (and I do mean severe) diarrhea throughout the entire weekend. And I thought it even more strange that in Columbus, I was having a hard time focusing, or maintaining that upbeat chatter that is the hallmark of a good facilitator.

Then Texas got canceled. And St. Louis got canceled. And Sacramento got canceled. I was having too tough a time at home even getting out of bed, much less trying to get on an airplane. My brain felt like one big fuzzball, with any semblance of organized thinking going right out the window. While I was living alone for the first time in many years, even my precious dogs were starting to turn into perpetual annoyances. Worst of all, the mortgage company was showing signs of serious lack of management. What in the hell was going on? What was wrong with me?

The statement, "No, I'm sorry, I'm booked up for the next several months," became my untruthful mantra. As the book began to soar in popularity, the calls for speaking engagements seemed to come with the rapidity of a machine gun, yet I was turning all of them down, including some on the very day I was to be there. (That always went over well.) More and more days were spent in bed, as more and more calls to have radio interviews were rejected. What was going on? What was wrong?

Doctor, Please?

One doctor after the other, one specialist after the other, but still no help. "Try this antidepressant." "Try this sleeping pill." "We can't find anything wrong with you."

Nothing wrong? I was dragging my rear end so far behind me that just the thought of speaking (which by now had become a thing of the past), or of maintaining the mortgage company, or even feeding my poor dogs sent me into major overwhelm.

Then there were the sweet and well-meaning friends who kept telling me in all kindness to read my book. "Lynn, you wrote it, why don't you practice it?" One more of those calls, and I'd put out a contract on whoever was on the other end of the phone.

Finally, in desperation, I contacted a friend who was a homeopathic practitioner. She properly diagnosed that, while I may not have had diabetes, my organs were responding as if diabetes was actually my problem. She put me on a strict diabetic diet, had me check my blood sugar constantly, and sure enough, I started to come out of the morass I had been in.

But why hadn't the doctors found this? What kind of gifts did my friend have that she could spot what was wrong? And even more important, *why* was it wrong? What could possibly be going on with me that would send me into a diabetic-like seizure, if I didn't have diabetes?

It wasn't long before I found out, or at least I thought I had found out. The appalling thing is that I was pleased.

My friend was able to gather information about the body, *from* the body, because she actually talked to the body. Although she was a medical specialist, she was also what many would call a "seer," something far beyond a psychic. She could talk with those who walked with me in the unseen, then, together with her own medical knowledge and whatever information she was getting from what I called "my troops" in the unseen, she'd come up with the answers that were finally getting me back on my feet. Or at least, almost back on my feet.

What startled me the most, though, was when she began telling me that my frequencies were being raised artificially in preparation for more experimentation on my body. And then came something about a "shamanic double." Huh? A what? But that's all the information I got, for a long, long time.

No matter, this gal was helping me out for the time being, at least. I stuck religiously to my diabetic diet, while my frequencies were being pushed up farther and farther. Night sweats became commonplace, and had nothing to do with menopause as that happening was most assuredly ancient history.

My poor adrenal glands were completely out of gas, but would kick back as long as I stayed on certain homeopathic supplements. Life seemed to be getting a bit better, but my energy level was nowhere near where it should be. I wanted more information, damn it, more than I was getting from my friend, but how to get the information or where to go for it was a puzzle. Nonetheless, I kept searching for answers any and every place I could, while also doing all I could to keep my highly successful mortgage company on its wavering feet.

Looking back on those first three years of strangeness, I see now how cleverly the information was being leaked to me from those in the unseen, through my friend. It was only as much as I needed to keep me feeling honored to be of service in this lofty scheme to bring more Light, and awareness, and awakening to mankind. "Oh, what fools we mortals be!" And what a bunch of BS!

After all, if my frequencies were being raised, then didn't that mean that other folks would benefit as a result? Wasn't the goal of all of us on this noble spiritual path to raise our frequencies? So I was helping, right? Seemed reasonable to me.

With this kind of muddled thinking, I was willing to suffer through the diabetic stuff that was, in fact, coming from organs being shut down, one by one, as they were being rebuilt in a higher frequency. Sure. That made sense. Good for me, look at what I'm doing for mankind. I had conveniently, and temporarily, forgotten about this "shamanic double" stuff, focusing on the "good for me" syndrome, instead. "I'll handle it, by God. Watch this! I'll handle it. Good for me!" Ho, ho ho!

The Age of the Swinger

Fortunately, during all of this strangeness, I was able to put back into practice the principles in *Excuse Me . . .* Life, in general, seemed to be much less stressful. Although I wasn't out mowing my acres of grass anymore or tossing balls for my pups, and surely not accepting any speaking engagements, I was able once again to have some real weekend fun working on my new book, the "Playbook" for *Excuse Me . . .* I was seeing friends more frequently, and living an almost normal life.

But that blasted "shamanic double" thing kept going around and around in my head, and I wanted more answers.

"How high are my frequencies to be raised?"

"What happens then?"

"Who's doing this?"

"Is it with my permission?"

"What do you mean shamanic double?"

"What's it for?"

"What are the benefits to the planet, or mankind, or for that matter, to me?"

"How long is this going to go on?" Etc., etc.

Questions, questions, questions. They were so prolific in my head, I started writing them down just to make them stop. Then, right in the midst of this frantic search for answers, I found something for which today I'm deeply grateful, but at the time—and for several years to come— proved to bring me one major disaster after the other.

"Well, what the hell. I've tried everything else, so why not try it? No, don't do this, you're going outside of Self. Anyhow, it's nothing but wishful thinking. Or maybe worse. Oh, who cares? If you might get an answer or two . . . maybe . . . well, why not! All right, do it, but in the name of Heaven, don't tell anyone!"

So I bought a pendulum. I called it my "swinger." Little did I know what a savage set-up this was to be for me, or how much pain it would cause. All I could see in my desperate search for answers was . . . answers!

"Wow! Wild! Fantastic! I'm home free. This really works. Now I can find out what's been happening to me, what I should do, what I should eat, take, or smell! Let's talk about the books. Let's talk about where to live. Let's talk about . . . oh hell . . . anything that might make me feel better."

Let me hasten to say that a pendulum, if properly used (and I do mean *V-E-R-Y* properly used), can be an incredible tool to providing a sense of knowing about one's self that might otherwise be unobtainable. But, like anything else from the unseen, including voices in one's head, or so-called channeled information through an individual, or the Ouija board, or Tarot cards, or runes, it can also be a shattering catastrophe to one's well-being. It surely was to mine. I fell for what was coming from that swinger, hook, line, and sinker, without giving a thought to anything about proper or improper use. Shoot, I'd ask a question, and get an answer. What could be so malicious about that? In truth, the maliciousness of what I was being fed never occurred to me.

What I didn't know at the time—to my great regret— was that a whole bunch of entities that were around me were working overtime, and oh, so happily, to provide me with answers that would best suit their needs and the fulfillment of our mutual contract that didn't have a damn thing to do with bringing Light to this plane, only research to them.

"Should I be taking this stuff suggested by my friend? And if so, is it the proper amount?"

"Yes, you should take it, but no, it is not the proper amount. Cut it back by *X*-amount. Or increase it by *X*-amount. Or, no, stop it all together."

That's when the true sickness of my body and mind really began. Not the horror that was yet to come: just the mental and physical sickness as the symptoms of advanced diabetes (that doctors continued to tell me I didn't have) seemed to progress with frightening speed. By now it was clear that I was not getting better, as I had so hoped. There was no question, I was getting worse, and it scared the holy hell out of me.

Both my homeopathic friend and my swinger continued to tell me that I was in the process of rapidly raising my frequencies. That information felt right to me, for how could anyone feel like I was feeling, have no medical symptoms, and not have something very unusual happening to them?

I knew enough about so-called spiritual enlightenment (and I say that so very guardedly) to believe that what was happening to me was simply something that I must have signed up for long ago, and that while it may be uncomfortable for a while, it would surely be to the benefit of all humanity. Once again, ho, ho ho!

"Swinger or guides, am I raising my frequencies for the benefit of mankind?" "Yes."

"Swinger or guides, is this process going to go on much longer?" "No."

"Swinger or guides, are you sure?" Big swing to the right for a major "Yes."

Swinger or guides "this," and swinger or guides "that." I felt comfortable in the knowledge that I was getting answers, answers that made me feel secure in what was happening to me, answers that I felt I needed . . . about my mortgage company, and book sales, and bodily changes, and, and, and . . .

"Swinger or guides, there seems to be something wrong with my dog, Lucy. Can you tell me what that is?" I wait until I think I've heard their answer in my thoughts, then verify that response with the swinger.

"My dog has a tumor!?" "Yes."

"Are you sure?" "Yes."

Naturally I flew into a panic, just the reaction the goons who were operating my swinger had wanted. I knew that such a negative emotion was against everything that was good for one's life, but my head was so muddled, and my body so exhausted, flipping to a more reasonable thought and feeling seemed to be as impossible as taking a Sunday drive to the moon.

I was calm when the veterinarian thought she saw a little black lump in the X-rays. After all, that's what had been predicted. The team of dog-doctors operated, and found nothing.

As long as I live, I will never forget the following day when I went in to get poor Lucy at the vet's. She had always had a palpable fear of cages, yet there she was in the cage, dejected, forlorn, and more miserable than I have ever seen any living creature in my entire life.

"Good for you, Lynn, good for you. You have just had your beloved dog sliced open for no reason at all. Maybe now you'll take a different look at that blasted swinger."

Everything in me said something was wrong with my using that swinger, but I kept going back for more answers. Everything in me said I was getting answers that made no sense, but I kept going back for more. Everything in me said to put the damn thing down. But I didn't.

A Short-Lived Respite

Soon I was to the point where, for months on end, I couldn't get out of bed except to feed the dogs and me. My bedroom TV became my only escape, as the physical exhaustion increased, and my once-healthy emotional state eroded to bare survival.

The requests to have radio interviews continued to be forwarded from my publisher, until I had to finally ask them to make some kind of excuse, and cut the requests off completely. When the phone would ring, I'd fly into a panic, irrationally wondering if it was a lawsuit for the mortgage business, or a request for a speaking engagement.

Nothing was making sense. I clung to the belief that this was all for the good of mankind. Good God! How in the bloody hell could anyone in their right mind continue to think that way? And that was the point. I was no longer in my right mind, not by a long shot.

Finally my homeopathic friend put her foot down and gently demanded that I start listening to her rather than to my still-too-trusted swinger. After a year and a half of bed, and garbled mind, and overwhelm, and confusion, I listened to her, and the recovery began, once again. At least, that's what I thought it was.

The *Playbook* was almost finished, and with the royalties coming in so nicely from *Excuse Me . . .* , I knew I could finally put the mortgage business aside. I made the excuse to my wonderful mortgage people that, because there were so many pressures on my time from the popularity of the book, that that's where my passion was now and that I needed and wanted to follow that passion.

For a brief while, as that business was in the process of being sold, I seemed to be back on track, finishing up the *Playbook*, doing a few radio interviews, and loving my dogs again. All seemed to be settling down. Maybe this unpleasantness was really coming to an end. Maybe I could have a life. Maybe I could move back to California. Maybe, maybe, maybe . . .

chapter three

the fairy tale
that is true

Once upon a time before time ever was, there was a void. Well, no, there was just a nothingness. Well, not really, there was no thing. Not nothing, but NO thing!

Creation for Dummies Like Me

It took the unpleasant shift from the first three-year segment of mild discomfort to the next three years of indescribable physical and emotional torture before I finally—*finally*—caught on that my swinger was being skillfully manipulated by a bunch of not-so-nice entities to cause me suffering of inconceivable proportions. But once I got the message, and learned what I needed to do to get truly accurate information from that little rock—instead of disaster—everything changed, and all the horribleness stopped. (Don't worry, I'll tell you how.)

At long last, I knew what was happening to me, and it was not pleasant. It had nothing to do with the exalted "back-of-the-hand-to-the-forehead" syndrome that I had clung to for so long about all the maaa-vel-ous things I was doing for the Light and for mankind. Oh no. It had to do with how I was being manipulated by a batch of out-of-this-universe goons that I wanted no part of.

Finally, but not soon enough, I found out how to stop the physical and emotional punishment I was experiencing. Needless to say, the relief was extraordinary.

In a short period of time, after I finally learned how to avoid interruption and/or manipulation of my swinger, I discovered not only what was happening to me, but what had been happening to mankind for untold eons, along with the exhilarating story of what is—I hope—to be coming down the pike for us all, very soon.

I found out how to stop the dreadful torture I had been going through in the second three years of my personal manipulation by forces I didn't want anywhere near me. Perhaps most important of all, I found out why this was happening. It was then, after the hell had stopped, that I knew (and was soundly told), that I had to pass this information on via a book.

"Are you out of your mind? Are you kidding? Who, in the name of God, is going to believe me? I'll be blacklisted with not only my own publisher, but with every publisher on this planet, not to mention all those trusting folks who have bought my books and so excitedly benefited from them. Isn't there another way? Oh please, isn't there?"

"No, this story must be told."

"Oh brother! Oh help! Oh no!"

Nevertheless, I started in, assembling piece by piece what I was "hearing" in my thoughts, and verifying what I was getting with my swinger as well as from copious books written and channeled long ago before things started heating up on our planet.

Is it accurate? Is it for real? All I can say is that no self-respecting entity from the dark would be caught relaying this kind information, for it is—to us, at least—most unbecoming to that large group of beings.

In truth, I don't really know if this magnificent story I'm about to relate is true. I only know that this is how I heard it and verified it to the best of my ability.

This is the story of creation. It is endearing, yet describes with a very broad brush why humanity has always had it so tough. As I have no desire, much less ability, to make a cosmic physics lesson out of this information, it comes to you as it did to me, in consummate simplicity.

Who cares if the myriad of finite details and nuances are missing? Who cares if the story is being passed onto me in more ungarnished verbiage than probably even God ever thought possible? Myth is, after all, just a way of taking an abstract thought and putting it into a digestible format.

And that's what this story is: a fairy tale with its foundation seated truth. At least, that's what I've been told.

The point of the story is that all of us, in all realities within this universe, have been put through a wringer of hell that we want no part of any longer. So, in less than nursery school jargon, this is the story about how we all got into this mess in the first place, along with the endearing story of how our universe was formed. But simplistic or not, without this little story—the essence of which I earnestly believe to be quite factual—nothing else in these pages would make any sense at all.

Some of this information was coming at me so fast, I don't remember a lot of what might be important. I wrote as much and as fast as I could in various sessions, but I was writing so rapidly, I couldn't read my scribbles. I've tried to pull as much of that information back as possible, but when you can't read what it is you want to ask about, what is there to ask? Ah well, here we go.

The No-Thing Moves

Some esoteric books say, " . . . and the no-thing

contemplated itself, and creation was born." Others say
". . . and there began indiscernible movement within the
no-thing."

What I got was that—and please, don't let me lose you
here—what I got was that the no-thing, before anything
ever was, was like a black hole ready to fall in on itself.
When that falling in finally happened, friction from the
movement of the falling was created, like a swinging
pendulum of a grandfather clock.

So as the no-thing fell in upon itself, it would go back
and forth, back and forth, until the actual movement of it,
through itself, created the friction.

Now, of course, the no-thing had no place to go,
because there was no such thing as "place," for space had
not yet been created. (Believe me, this is just as mind-
boggling to me as it probably is to you.) So, because the
no-thing had no place to go, it just kept falling in on itself,
back and forth, back and forth, as it was somehow rooted
in the middle.

Back and forth, back and forth. There was no thought,
it was not intelligent by our standards, but something was
indeed happening in this spaceless, timeless non-reality as
the no-thing would stop (for even a few micro-seconds of
time as we know it to be) and then once again fall back in
on itself.

As the no-thing was swinging in microscopic,
infinitesimal fluctuations back and forth, the friction that

was being created eventually caused a spark. But not just one spark, two came off of the no-thing.

During its swings from one side to the other (I don't know how else to describe it), the first spark was emitted from the friction. Then, as it once again fell back in on itself and swung to the other side, another spark was emitted.

Now here's the point to this whole story: what had happened was that the first spark was of one frequency, and the second spark was of another, much higher frequency. And if the one we call God, that came from the second higher frequency spark knows why this strange event ever happened, he's not telling.

At any rate, now we had our first two sparks in the Isness, the potential for the beginnings of something, but of what?

As countless eons passed, and more sparks of different frequencies were discharged from the no-thing, the first two sparks began to develop awareness, of each other, of the other sparks, and eventually of themselves.

I need to stop here and reiterate once again, that while I have some very descriptive books on creation, and dimensions, and the original black hole and how it got that way, and the conception of entities and Selves and artificial intelligence and what we're made of and so on, all of that thoroughly fascinating information is not why I'm writing this book.

This little story is not only the Reader's Digest version of creation (that would be putting it mildly), it is the truth in fictionalized form to give the necessary background to where we're going in these pages. It is the truth, but a long, long way from the bewildering, incomprehensible physics of how this universe, in which we live, came to be. All right, that said, on we go.

The First Two Sparks

Bit by bit, over countless eons, as our first two sparks were growing in their strange new awareness of each other and their surroundings, they were also becoming aware of their desire for "more." More what? Well, I can only speak for one of the sparks, for that's where my story comes from. We won't give him a name yet, just Number Two, who was born of the highest frequency off of the no-thing's come-back swing.

Remember, there was no Light, which is created from friction, there was only dark. Yes, the no-thing had made just enough stir to create the friction that hatched that first spark of Light in the nothingness, and soon the no-thing had gotten up enough steam to hatch that brighter spark. To this day, there is none brighter.

The first spark, existing in its lower frequency, became known to those of us on earth as Lucifer (and many other names), and the second spark, *of the highest frequency in all of existence*, we'll call Abraham, although that is not his real name. In fact, we'll have some fun and call him "Abe." But fun or no, this is the entity that we, who are within this universe, call God.

As these two sparks grew in awareness of themselves, and played, and tested, and experimented in the discovery of what they were, they found they could create. Brother Lucifer was the first to bring substance into their reality, and before long (well, you know what I mean), he was making universes, places where his other brothers who had also been sparked off of the no-thing, could enter and play and create as well. Abe, who knew he was different from his brother, just watched. And waited.

In time—that didn't exist—Lucifer was not only populating universes with his brothers, but had found he could create duplicates of himself, sparks from his own spark, or what some call "pinch-offs." Abe didn't go in for creating pinch-offs as his brother was doing. Since all brothers he had were of lesser vibrations than he was, the only way he could create "company" for himself would be from pinch-offs. But still, he watched. And waited.

Creation was now well under way, all from beings that were of a lower frequency than Abe! These beings were either first-born sparks from the no-thing and all of a lower frequency than Abe who was the absolute highest, or they were pinch-offs from some of that lower frequency group.

Abe had no "friends," no companions who were of his own frequency. He had created no pinch-offs, and had none of his frequency for company. So, he just watched. And waited.

Abe watched his brother and all of the other sparks of lower frequencies that had been born of the no-thing, and all of their pinch-offs (all lower frequencies than Abe), start to play around with building little universes, all the same, all consistent with what had been created before. And far too many of them.

Chaos was becoming the name of the game. Universes sprung up all over the place, all being populated by lower frequency entities. Universes were developing so fast with all of Lucifer's brothers and their pinch-offs playing around, that their limited space—which was not even a known thing then—was becoming threatened (I know, we think of space as limitless. 'Tis not!) and Abe just watched. And waited.

All of these many new entities of lower frequency than Abe, within and without their universes, were alive, but without Life. Granted, they carried the divine spark of the no-thing, the electrical vibrational energy of the force from which they had been hatched. But still, they did not have Life as we know it to be within this universe.

In fact, they didn't give a hoot about Life, because they didn't even know about it. All they cared about was matching what "this guy" had done, or "that guy." Fights broke out: who could be or go where? . . . for how long? . . . then what? . . . who could find room to create next? . . . how big? . . . and then what?

And so, out of sheer necessity, some of the oldest sparks that had birthed after Lucifer (not pinch-offs, but the originals born of the no-thing), were asked to form a governing body to oversee and regulate who could do what within their limited area: who could build what, and what the terms had to be in order to qualify for any new enterprise. The group was called then, as is to this day, "The Elders," all comprised of entities of lower vibration than Abe.

Our Home Becomes

This universe, meaning everything we see out there as stars and black holes and nebulas, etc., is a package of containment. It is not endless, and is held in place (although still expanding) by the entity that started the whole thing in the first place. But let's get back to our story.

Abe watched what was happening all around him with interest, but not with action. He watched these small containments we call universes being created by his brother and others, and he watched the original sparks from the no-thing hatch more and more of themselves to go into these universes. And he watched as the Elders approved all of the ventures, every last one.

Abe saw that all of the originators seemed to be doing the same thing, over and over. They'd make a new universe from thought. Then, once their universe was created, that was the end of anything new. Not one thing was happening that was new, not even from new generations of sparks that were being created from the old sparks. Over and over, it was the "same old, same old."

So one day (oh sure), Abe decided to step up to the plate for his turn. He wanted to see what could be created that would not only be different in its inception, but would house beings that would never be satisfied with just creating more sparks of themselves. Unlike his brother, Abe was an explorer, a searcher, a seeker, so why shouldn't whatever he created be the same? That way, who knew what might happen, or what might be created that would be truly unprecedented?

Now here's where the story gets a little tacky.

Everything that exists, be it just blobs of energy as were being created then, or a rock as we know it to be today, every single thing that lives produces waste of some sort. So, after eons of seeing that nothing new was happening with his brother's creations or with the creations that were now coming from his brother's relatives, Abe decided to try something different.

By this time, because of the chaos being generated by these thousands of young whipper-snapper entities running around all over the Isness, the Elders were becoming concerned. Too much was happening too fast, so they decided to clamp down. They had been given this authority by everyone except Abe (who had abstained), and they took their assignment seriously.

Frankly, all of this Elder approval business seems really dumb to me, since all of the projects were basically the same. Nevertheless, before Abe could begin his unprecedented project, he had to get approval from this new governing group. Though the Elders thought his idea to be preposterous, they agreed, with conditions.

Abe wanted approval to gather much of the waste materials that were beginning to stack up throughout the Isness, put those materials into one place to be enveloped and watched over by himself, and see what would happen. Apparently, because what space they had to live in was so confined, and because in that confinement the wastes were becoming a major problem, Abe got instant approval, though his seemingly irresponsible idea was ridiculed by all.

And so began our universe with its many dimensions and realities and time frames. But the truth is, we all started from the wastes of entities who were—every single one of them—of a lower vibration than Abe, but still of magnificent presence.

Because forming universes was new to Abe, he had been told by the Elders that his brother must assist him, or at least be involved in this project, somewhat like a watchdog, to insure that nothing would happen that might adversely affect the reality in which they all now lived.

Abe agreed, but still decided to do this experiment his own way as best he could, without alerting either the Elders or his brother. He asked many of his own pinch-off sparks, which by now he had emitted for company, to help him out. All eagerly agreed. They knew Abe was different, and that his idea may just produce something wholly unexplored and unknown. So they all hopped on the bandwagon.

Unlike the manner in which his brother had simply "thought" universes into existence, Abe created a little womb of the Light of himself, placed the waste products into it much like the use of a scientist's petri dish, wrapped it with himself, and waited.

For a while, the Elders kept close tabs on Abe's experiment, but as time wore on and nothing happened, they tired of their watch and turned the safeguarding over to Abe's brother. "As long as it stays contained," they said to Abe and his brother, "you may proceed. But the minute it gets out of hand, we're pulling the plug."

The Wayward Little Kid

All who were involved with the project knew that the slough-off material placed inside the womb had a lower frequency than Abe. They were concerned as to what this mix of the highest known frequency, Abe, and the lower frequencies of most of the slough-off matter would bring. Would it last? Would it evaporate? Would it melt? Would it explode? Would it eat itself?

As the lower vibrational slough-off materials heated in the intensity of Abe's high vibrational Light, a biology started. Atoms were formed from the friction of so many mis-matched frequencies.

Then finally various forms of mass—which is nothing more than Light that's been lowered in frequency—began to form. No one had ever seen anything like this before. Substance! Mass! Amazing!

Rocks, which were actually microscopic sand-pebbles, came first and spread so rapidly that Abe and his team wondered how they were going to keep them contained. Innately they knew that what was happening in this little womb was the beginning of something extraordinary, but just what that something was, they had no idea. They only knew that more space was needed in which to let it all happen, or the whole thing could collapse.

There was, at that time, a new breed of entity which had been created from the no-thing that no one understood, and for the most part, everyone but Abe ignored. Abe called them "space particums." There were known to be only three in all of the Isness, and they were also known to be highly, highly independent.

These little space particums were known to be the most spontaneous and powerfully creative beings in existence, and Abe desperately wanted one for his project. Imagine! A being that could burst ideas into being that were based on no known form of existence; the ultimate form of creativity! That was for Abe. Good grief, if you could create like a space particum, you'd never be as bored as his brother or his brother's relatives had long since become.

Abe wanted to be like the space particum, for if he was, then all limitations of creation would be removed. But since he couldn't do that, the next best thing was to catch one, and invite it in.

Abe told only a select few about his hair-brained idea, and surely not his brother. In great secrecy they began their search for this strange entity. They searched in all the existing universes, and in the voids, and were about to give up when . . . they found one. They had found one of the three known space particums.

Needless to say, Abe was elated, and quickly sold the amazing little thing on his wild scheme. Abe told the space particum that his project was running out of room to expand, and asked for its help. Since the space particum had just been flitting around the Isness doing a lot of nothing, it readily agreed to accept the challenge to participate in Abe's venture.

Before long, the new arrival knew there was a problem brewing inside the womb. If the project was to survive, the womb had to expand, and expand fast. Abe could accommodate that request to some degree, but not to the extent the space particum knew would be necessary.

So, the space paritcum took over, expanding itself, and expanding itself, and expanding itself to monstrous proportions within the womb until—Whammo! The Big Bang happened, not just with the linings of the womb, but with all the little particles and tidbits that had taken shape inside of it! The space particum had saturated everything within the womb, as well as the womb itself, and everything, all at the same time, expanded, including the microscopic pebbles.

To the amazement of everyone involved, the little space particum had also found new forms of life that no one knew existed inside the womb, not even Abe. Those too expanded, with each localizing itself into various dimensions, depending on the vibrational frequency they had been spawned from in the first place.

The expansion was so monumental, it created fires, and gases, and more internal explosions, and discharges, and suns from the pebbles, and . . . Well, you get the idea.

Thus was born the first, and to this very day, the only universe ever created from the highest vibrational frequency of entity ever birthed in all of the Isness, and who still is the one who wraps us in his frequency of high vibrational love. The Elders didn't know what had hit them, but the nightmare—for them—had begun.

This Thing Called "Life"

The intent of the original experiment had always been—and still is—to create beings of free will, regardless of their dimensional reality; beings who would not be just clones of the original sparks, but who would desire to become their own creative source, beings who desired to be individualized, no matter how that was to be accomplished, or how long it would take.

In working toward this lofty goal, it soon became apparent that all of the developing creatures within this now expanding womb had something that no being in any of the other universes had—an electromagnetic field. Where had it come from? What caused it? Why had that happened?

The answer lies somewhere in the friction caused by Abe's highest known frequency and the lower frequencies of most of the slough-off materials.

The higher (and highest) frequency entity was wrapping the lower frequency particles with its high vibration of what we would now call 100 percent pure Light and ceaseless love, creating a kind of cloaking that we have come to call Spirit around the developing life forms.

Take these two things, the life sparks being created from the slough-off materials which, while mostly lower in frequency, were nonetheless divine, intelligent, and aware, and merge all of that with the high vibrational frequency of the womb's creator, Abe, and you have something utterly unique in all of existence. Life! Ongoing Life, never before known in all of the Isness.

Gradually more and more of Abe's team emitted their own life sparks, their pinch-offs, into this extraordinary new womb to create unheard-of, totally unknown breeds of entities. These new entities may have been formed originally from lower frequency properties, but they had now merged with the highest vibrational life sparks in all of the Isness. And each and every one of them had this mysterious high vibrational mantle we now call Spirit.

Poor Lucifer. Whether in light bodies or in more solid mass as we are now, the new entities that continued to birth inside this womb were baffling to him. They were unequaled and unheard of, for they could think for themselves, create for themselves within their dimensional boundaries, become who and what they wanted to be, and never cease to exist, all the attributes we now call Life with a capital "L." Not just living, but Life.

Abe's brother watched, and desperately wanted what Abe was creating. In fact, all of The Others wanted to participate and share in what was happening inside of this universe. They became insanely jealous of what was forming here, and vowed amongst themselves that they would go to any lengths to obtain these mysteries that had never before been witnessed outside of Abe's creation . . . this thing they had never known to be possible, called Life.

As our universe continued to expand—thanks to the ever vigilant little space particum—into more glorious and unheard-of realities with conceptions of magnificent forms of Life on multitudinous planets in varying realms, The Others, those lower frequency entities that we now call "dark" who lived outside of our universe, decided to take matters into their own hands.

Abe's big brother was obsessed with obtaining the radiance and originality of what his younger brother had either knowingly or unknowingly created: entities of Life who could think on their own and fend for themselves, entities of Life who could live in many different realities if they chose to, entities of Life who never ceased to exist, entities of Life who passioned to evolve into the high frequency of pure love, which was the hallmark of the maker of the womb in which they lived.

Not one in the entire universe ever gave a thought to returning to the lower frequency residue from which they may have sprung. Not one. Not ever.

But good old big brother was becoming a force to be reckoned with. The one we call Lucifer, mighty divine entity that he was, was ticked off and starting to cause trouble. He was resentful, he was covetous, and he was intensely powerful.

Lucifer wanted this thing called Life for his entire family of spawned sparks . . . and their families . . . and their families. And the only way he knew how to get that was to infiltrate Abe's universe in any way he could, working towards the eventual overthrow of Abe's dominance. After all, wasn't he, Lucifer, the appointed "watchdog" of this coveted experiment?

Big Brother Plots

And so the war that we have heard so much about, the war between the Light and the dark, had begun. Yes, that same war is heating up now to gigantic proportions, but it began oh so very long ago, when our universe was still in diapers.

At the outset, it began rather slowly. Oh sure, it might have taken a few billion years for things to really act up, but that's nothing in the non-time frame of a bunch of old and bored gods from the "outside."

Lucifer's plan evolved. Soon he and his troops were placing some of their own kind inside the expanding womb, but Lucifer, himself, had now been banned. The

Elders had become so fascinated with this new and expanding "thing" Abe had created, that they agreed to Abe's request to withdraw Lucifer as "watchdog." They, the Elders, would watchdog this thing themselves, thank you very much.

So now it was his brother's relatives who were entering, not Lucifer himself. No matter. Lucifer figured that whether he was allowed in or not, he would oversee and monitor the conflict that was to come by having "his men" infiltrate Abe's universe in every way possible. He rightly figured that since the womb was expanding so rapidly, sparks from his family coming in would be completely overlooked. In fact, he reasoned, they would even help to fill the ongoing expansion by creating new realities for more sparks to fill.

Abe knew that sparks from the "outside" were coming in in droves, but for a while, at least, he felt that was all right. After all, what had been created within this womb had come mostly from lower vibrations in the first place, so what could be the harm?

Calculating the numbers that would be required to render a change from the then current high vibration of Light to a lower frequency where he could be in control, Lucifer devised a brilliant plot to have his people enmesh themselves in this thing that was being called "Spirit," which surrounded every being inside the womb, regardless of reality.

Dear God! What's Happening to Us?

The plan was that The Others would entice those in all realms who had just left their bodies for a new experience (what we would call death) into believing that they could more quickly fulfill their desire to become like their creator by allowing these "special" beings (Lucifer's buddies) to help guide them along in their next incarnations. For even then, as now, no being throughout the entire universe could incarnate who did not have a team to guide them. But that was only one approach for Abe's clever brother.

Next, Lucifer would send hoards of his own into this womb disguised as the original sparks that had emanated from Abe. They would be able to fool the inhabitants in all realities into thinking that they—The Others—were the original grand pinch-offs from Abe offering to be of service as guides to entities in all realities. From those vantage points, Lucifer knew his team could gain supremacy over almost every incarnate within Abe's universe.

And finally, they would infiltrate the mix of entities, or minute parts of entities that have always made up the consciousness mix of a being within this universe, whether from the Pleiades in Light body, or from one of the Earths in solid body. (There are three dimensions of Planet Earth: ours is third dimension, one is fifth dimension, and the other is seventh dimension.)

If Lucifer could infiltrate any of these areas of existence, then he could take control and eventually find the means to give his own people this precious new thing called Life.

True, all beings within this universe were seeking to be UNcontrolled, but if Abe's brother had his way, eternal Life outside of this existence would become a reality for all of his people.

Change the consciousness, change the mix of their guidance, and change the primary entity of these beings who were now proliferating so abundantly and eagerly inside this detestable new womb, and "control of the Isness will be mine once again." That became Lucifer's mantra, one which he would go to any lengths to accomplish.

Taking Up Residence

Gradually and carefully, so as not to cause disruption, more and more of the growing number of lower frequency entities from the outside began to take up residence within this universe of Life. If they could find ways to blend into the various realities, then they could also find ways to incorporate themselves into the lives of beings within the various realities. Once they had done that, they surely would be able to crack the secrets of this Life thing, and find out how to develop it for themselves.

As time went on, the presence of The Others within our universe grew out of proportion to those of high frequency Light. They were even founding their own realities in what we would call star systems.

The Others were determined to have this place for their own, but no matter how much they infiltrated, or created their own places of existence, how to survive in this expanding womb of high frequency Light was baffling, and they were beginning to accept the fact that, if they wanted this Life thing for themselves, in their own realms, they would have to find a way to sustain that Life outside of this universe. There had to be a way, there just had to be. They would not give up until they had found the answer. They would not give up.

Oh-So Splendid Maneuvers

Over countless generations of study, The Others worked tirelessly to find ways to craft a being of Life for themselves. They devised what appeared to be outwardly harmless ways to infiltrate systems of reality in our universe. They attempted all manner of clonings in hundreds of different realities in vain attempts to recreate themselves with a Spirit, or soul, when all the evidence was supporting the fact that a cloned being could never, ever have a Spirit or soul, meaning Life. And it still can't!

(When any human ever gets to the far side of the moon, they'll be blown away by the experiments taking place there to recreate our species with souls. It ain't pretty, and of course, it ain't gonna happen.)

Eventually The Others decided the low-third dimension that held the human creature would be the easiest reality to penetrate. To begin with, the human body was a creation unlike anything throughout the entire universe, holding every secret of existence since the first spark from the no-thing.

Adding to that, the human guide system was a fairly easy one to worm into, since the human requires a minimum of three guides from the unseen in order to embody (more than most realities). All they had to do was become friends with a human during a particular lifetime or two or three, then offer their "caring" guidance to that being for its next incarnation, and presto! They were in.

The Others found ways to gain access to the human's consciousness in order to influence his decisions in life. That was major!

The Others found ways to become fully human, with what we call the "higher self" coming directly from themselves. That too was major, even though they couldn't take the human, meaning its soul, outside of our universe.

In fact, almost every day (which there was not), The Others were finding tantalizing new ways to influence this species, to control this species, and to overthrow this species for their own benefit.

Their numbers incarnating directly into human bodies were increasing rapidly. The human was where it was happening. The human was the easiest and most promising species over which they could gain control. Surely, the human was the species that would ultimately show them how to have Life.

Of course, The Others had not planned that those of their own kind incarnating into the human body would want to stay here. That was a real "oops!"

They had not planned on defections, yet it was happening.

They had not planned on desertions from their own realities due to the enormous pleasures of the higher frequencies of Life, once in a human body or anywhere else. Yes, this was a problem, but they would overcome it with increased attention.

But now, focus on the human became all consuming to The Others. Surely this was the creature that would break open their stalemated desire for Life.

Surely this was the creature that would bring them into ultimate power throughout the universe.

Indeed, this human being that was mostly created from their own lower frequencies, but that was now infused with the Light of Life, offered so much potential for them to step into their desire for Life, that their focus on our third-dimension reality became fanatical. And still is.

Except for those who have chosen otherwise.

chapter four

the birth
and the deal

Data was being downloaded into me now faster than I
could verify with my now-trusted swinger. I had just been
through the second three years of such incomprehensible
hell that . . . oh well. Enough for now. The torture was
over. Now it was down to the book, but good lord guys,
ease up on the flow of input, or I'll end up getting
nothing.

Information, along with astounding details, was
pouring into me faster than I could write it down for
swinger verification. Most of what came through I was
able to verify as soon as I wrote it down. Some other
things were apparently not quite as clear, for my swinger
would show me, "No, that's not quite what we wanted to
say . . . try it more like this. Yes, yes, that's it."

I had always been fascinated by our origins (well

shoot, hasn't everyone?) and had a deep wonder as to why in heaven's name we, the human race, were continuing to go through so much turmoil. Good God, hadn't we been around long enough to make some serious corrections? I knew damn well that we *had* been around long enough, but why hadn't those changes happened?

When the story of The Others unfolded, it became all too clear as to why we, as humanity, had not made the changes we had all so desperately been seeking. And it was also all too clear that we had a fight on our hands, not just for our human race, but for our entire universe.

"So okay, guys, is it this so-called birth thing that's going to turn us around? For real?"

The answer never wavered from a consistent "Yes!" And so it began with me, the story of "The Birth."

What Is It?

This thing we're going into is known and called by many names in various religious circles, but what it all boils down to is that Abe finally got fed up with The Others messing around so drastically with his creation. So he and his team devised a plan long, long ago, that would say to The Others:

"All right, brothers of the no-thing, and brothers of those brothers, you've had your fun, now enough is enough. You will either decide to integrate fully into the Light, meaning give up completely the low-frequency origins from which you were birthed, or get outta here for all time."

Abe's plan was gradually and oh, so carefully formulated. There would be created within the universe a mammoth energy wave of such enormously high frequency proportions that the force of this wave, as it slowly made its way throughout the entire universe, would overpower many, kill many, and force a great many to leave the universe all together.

The wave, which was not really a wave at all but a newly created entity, was named Psi.

Oh yes, it was a very real, very dynamic, and hugely powerful living entity that was to act as a force to sweep the universe with its high frequency. But it was also a supremely intelligent power. I spoke just once with that entity, an experience I will never, ever forget. Not even Abe, who created the entity in the first place, seemed to possess the clout and intensity of authority of that being (though of course, he did!). I shiver even now as I think of the brief exchange we had.

Two hundred years ago; that's when Psi began his voyage across the universe, raising frequencies, creating havoc, cleaning house wherever he went.

Some realities have been less severely affected than others due to the already high dimensional frequencies in which they live. But all realities, in all dimensions, have been strenuously challenged because all have been infiltrated by The Others whose frequency range rarely comes close to Psi's aggressive wave that was now sweeping across their homelands.

Abe called the times that would come, as a result of this high-powered housecleaning, "The Birth." Frankly, I might have been inclined to call it "The Preparation," or "Operation Go Get 'em," something with a bit more of General Patton's chutzpah. But "The Birth" it was.

And so the blueprints for this massive offensive came off the drawing boards centuries ago, and went into full-scale execution. Everyone involved knew it was going to be a rough ride. Abe was, after all, somewhere around a mind-boggling 50th-dimension entity. The highest dimension to date that held Life in our universe was somewhere around 12th dimension. Abe's brother was somewhere around a 45th dimension. Psi was programmed for around a 15th-dimension entity.

And then there's us.

But now the infiltration by The Others had caused this universe too much harm. Even the so-called Elders who still controlled and regulated so many of the happenings within our new universe knew they were in trouble. But since they were all members of The Others, they did their best to balance their sympathetic agreement with what their brothers of lower frequencies wanted to obtain, with what they—the Elders—felt might be a give-and-take in order to maintain their positions of power.

No matter, Psi was now on his way. His journey would take him across every variation of dimensional space within the universe. In perfect organization, Psi started at the top of our universe, and began, oh so carefully and meticulously, to work his way down to where he is today, all the way down into our Milky Way galaxy, down to our solar system, and now flooding all over our earth.

We may be bringing up the rear, but we're sure getting the worst of it, simply because of our lower frequencies.

Last on the List

Although Psi has, by now, made his presence felt all over our universe, let's just talk about us, the third dimensional species known as human that The Others would so dearly like to control and clone, and where Psi is now focusing all of his energies.

How long has it been since the human being has felt much joy on an on-going basis?

How long has it been since the majority of humans have had a will to live, or a tenacious love of life?

How long has it been since the human knew that he was here on this planet to have fun—not strife—but fun, and excitement, and good times, and to enjoy life?

Has it ever been? Sadly no, it has not. So what happened? Where did it get so off base?

The grim yet exciting truth is that our little old species,

the human, has the potential as none other throughout this entire universe will ever have, to become a grander breed than has ever been known since the beginning of creation, holding within its being the knowledge of every single happening in manifested existence since and before the beginning of time.

Hello??? Are you kidding? Take a pill, calm down, that can't be right. Us? The poor beleaguered, inconsequential little human being? Like me? You gotta be kidding!

No. There is no kidding to this. It is a universal truth that what we are is where it's at. But we gotta put everything we have into this birth thing, or we'll be waiting (are you ready for this?) for another 35 million years with another 35 million zeros behind it for such an event to ever happen again.

Thank you just the same, but I've already had enough, and have no intention of waiting that long to have some long-delayed, long-overdue fun.

Oh, Little Button!

I really need to voice a few things in my own defense of all this weirdness. Truthfully, it wasn't so many years ago that if anyone had ever approached me with the things I'm writing about now, I would have told them where they could stick it.

Religion made little impact on me, (my gold commemorative cross of seven years in the Episcopal church choir notwithstanding). Sure, there was probably a force of some kind, but who really cared? If it was, it was. If it wasn't, it wasn't. Who cared?!

Then, in the depths of a long breakup of many, many years, something happened. I wanted more answers to What and Who I was, and I wanted them now. It was as if I had been turned inside-out. I was different. I felt different. I still ran my mortgage business. I still swore with intolerance at incompetent, unprofessional people. But something was different.

All I'm saying is that, hey, I'm no different from you.

I've been through alcoholism and Alcoholics Anonymous.

I've been through lack to the point of eating dog food.

I've been through both hating and loving my parents and various other relatives.

I've created companies that have had some horrible failures, along with those that have had some amazing successes.

There's not much I haven't been through, except maybe having kids. There are few of the ups and downs of life that are strangers to me. Damn few!

So. That having been said, here I am writing about creation, and good guys and bad guys, and vibrational frequencies, and "hearing" thoughts which some would call channeling, and saying that I'm getting it all from the guy who created this universe in the first place, and talking about what kind of trouble I'm told our particular species is in, and . . . oh God, have I lost it?

This is not the old "me" that I have known for so long. This is not the "Button" Grabhorn in pigtails that used to love playing cowboys and Indians, or loved belly-flopping down a snow-packed street, or loved kicking around the heady fragrances of fall, but then somehow turned uncertain, and unsure. Well yes, I'm afraid it is, one and the same.

I'm just a human being who has gone through the conventional trials of living that all of us have experienced, and then for some reason, has become involved with a whole lot more, coming out with some sort of "message" that needed to be told.

"Hell's bells," I said to myself. "If it will help us turn this mess around and help us soon, then go ahead and tell it. Who cares what anyone thinks!" (Well . . . ?!)

So no matter what kind of a kook you may think I am, I'm going ahead to tell it like I got it.

This "Birth" Thing

Call it what you will (as most religions do), but just know that a rather revolutionary change is about to come over not only our reality, but the entire universe. It's called "The Birth."

Abe and crew had to figure out some way to rid his stunning creation of the covetous beings who were doing all they could to suck Life out of his universe. He had openly allowed their participation in the beginning, without full awareness of the breakdown that was to come. But in fact, he didn't have much choice.

They, The Others, have been unsuccessfully attempting to clone beings with Spirit from all realities, since this universe began. And still are.

They, The Others, have taken parts of beings from every reality to experiment with, and still are.

They, The Others, have become guides to incarnates in many realities, and still are.

They, The Others, have become the dominate consciousness of beings, and still are.

They, The Others, have found ways to temper all frequencies of joy in order to lower the incarnate's frequency closer to their own, making a miserable life for that incarnate, and still are.

They, The Others, have found ways to bend the minds of incarnates in almost every reality (some realities have overcome that domination), and still are.

They, The Others, have found ways to meld into every reality throughout this entire universe, and still are, particularly our own.

So Abe—the one many of us call "God"—and his devoted troops began to formulate a plan to shake loose the growing domination of The Others. First, though, a sizable group of entities from inside of this womb would have to *want* to choose Life. There would have to be a way to instill in all realities the realization that there was hope beyond where they were in their present Nows.

But let's just talk about us, us human guys where all the attention is, because we not only hold the secret of Life, as do entities in all realities of this universe, but we also hold in our bodies the entirety of all that is or ever was or will be within our universe, and before.

This Birth Thing

So just exactly what is this Birth thing? What is it going to accomplish, and how?

When is it going to happen?

What will it feel like?

Who will know it's happened, or is happening?

And what is going to be this grandiose, predicted result?

How on earth do I describe what I've been told?

A new world (earth)?

A new dimension?

A new type of human? Oh, sure, tell me another story.

How do I describe what we need to do to bring this event about? Well, all I can do is what my daddy used to say, just "run the flag up the pole, Honey, and see who salutes!" Okay, Pop, here goes.

These paragraphs that I wrote from my *Playbook* probably sum up the anticipated event about as well as anything else I could write:

> "Prophets, seers, and even biblical writers have foretold this time for ages. According to their ancient interpretations, sometimes with revelations of apocalyptic horrors, sometimes with visions of the end of time, sometimes with prophecies of rapture beyond imagination, they could see that mankind was in for unimaginable alterations.
>
> "While these seers were all close in their predictions, none can claim the brass ring, for what none of those visionary souls could grasp were the Whys of these times, or the physics that will—or will not—cause this event to become a reality.
>
> "Will it work? Will centuries of planning and maneuvering pay off? Will mankind birth itself into a new reality and a new species of divinity?
>
> "The call is out, and every single one of us on this planet has gotten that call. This is it. The time is now. It's either you-know-what or get off the pot, which in divine terms translates into something like we had best get our act together, or we're going to be left behind."

Since at this moment we all seem to be quite human, let's not worry about the rest of the universe; let's just zero in on us guys here. The rest of the gang out there will either make it or not, as they choose.

This birth thing that's coming down—probably sometime before 2012—is going to shove us into another dimension. No, not all of us, because many of us will remain in fear and struggle, without realizing that there is, indeed, a way out, which is what this book is about.

This birth thing is everything that The Others want to avoid, for it will mean they have lost their battle for Life. Oh, not all of them, but the majority won't be able to participate, because their frequencies would be an even greater mismatch than they are now.

This birth thing is going to act like a filtering system for everyone, but most especially for those still playing around with any of The Others, which is now totally unnecessary. And that bunch, the folks who will be left behind, aren't going to be real fond of the world they live in after this birth thing comes down.

On the other hand, those who have taken the initiative to boot these suckers (and that's not just play on words) out of our lives for good will find the going to be much easier in the midst of all the commotion that's going on around us now.

This birth thing will shape up to look as if a whole bunch of folks have died. But since that can't happen within this universe (death to the human is just an illusion . . . always has been), the truth is that they will have bumped "up" into the next dimension of earth that already exists.

This birth thing is about a new universe, lacking the control of The Others.

Planet Two

The point of the birth is to create a means to dump The Others, for all time. They so desperately want what we have, they are doing everything in their power, right now, to crash this event that will provide for hundreds of thousands a new world, a new life of Life, a new reality of beauty and joy. That's right, beauty and joy, I don't know how else to say it (though I'm not entirely sure just what that means).

In years to come, after the initial event happens, more entities who have chosen the Light will follow, and then more, and then more. So if you don't zoom outta here when this thing comes down, not to worry. You can zoom out later, something which I would most strongly suggest you do.

Is all of this just a hopeful dream?

Life . . . as long as we desire it to be?

Dreams that will manifest with far greater ease?

Hardships and conflicts that will become a thing of the past?

Amazing health?

Businesses and work endeavors that will benefit all?

No, this is not just a hopeful dream, and scientists already know of the existence of another planet Earth in the sixth dimension. It's what I call Planet Two.

Right now, there are somewhere around twenty million humans there who come and go in lifetimes as they choose.

(Can you imagine, an earth with only twenty million people on it?) And that earth is just like ours, only unsoiled.

Yes, there are still churches, at least a few of them. And there are cars, and planes, and trains, and schools, and universities, and movies, and theaters, and opera, and restaurants, and sporting events (sorry, no football), and most of the things we enjoy here. Even a few malls.

What there is NOT, however, are people being manipulated by The Others. So the free will that we were designed to have is an absolute truth on Planet Two, an accepted given, not just something we read about in utopian self-help books.

People on Planet Two truly love their lives, they treasure their creativity, they no longer live with a sense of separation or aloneness, and perhaps most importantly, they live without wars, or starvation, or atrocities.

People on Planet Two are no longer plagued by emotions of low vibrations, which is what we're all getting socked with so violently now from The Others. Emotions like fear, and anger, and depression, and resentment, all nicely (and erroneously) wrapped up in the belief we've come to swallow that this is just the human condition. What an unconscionable bunch of bunk!

I don't want to start sounding like some of the so-called flower children from the sixties who glorified "peace and love and joy" stuff. Humans will always require a certain level of challenge just to keep them growing and expanding. But frankly, "peace and love and joy" is very close to what we'll be experiencing on this sixth-dimension Earth, providing we dump our current baggage, soon!

Oh, and by the way, we'll still have money, but it will no longer be a symbol of success; just a physical manifestation of energy and a means of exchange and sharing.

There will be no wages as we know them now, for everyone's role and contribution in society will be of importance, and honored.

The Ballroom Or The Bar

Sometimes I have to laugh at the analogies I get, either as pictures or in thought, or both. This one's a doozy.

When I asked what would be the difference in the years following the birth between Planet Two and the one we're in now, I was very clearly shown a magnificent ballroom filled with merry people, fun waiters, lovely music, and dancing couples that had to be straight from Central Casting.

"I presume this is Planet Two?"

"Yes."

Then came the picture of the dirtiest, grungiest barroom from back in the old West, with yucky, drunken dudes hanging all over the bar, fights going on all over the place, and of course the bartender just standing around nonchalantly drying his beer glasses.

"Oh come on," I said. "You're telling me that this is supposed to be what it's going to be like here on this planet we're on now, after this birth thing happens?"

"Yes, that's what we're telling you."

Well now, that gave me some pause for thought, but from there unfolded the rest of the story, and I was spellbound.

After the birth, The Others will be able to have full control of this, our current planet, almost as they do now, but with far less resistance than they are currently experiencing.

There will be no more cosmic teachers and very few human teachers of the Light.

There will be very few books published to promote well-being, and fewer still of the truly devoted religious ministry to turn to.

Corruption will be the name of the game everywhere, from governments down to local authorities. I get the feeling that if we think it's bad now, this is just the tip of the iceberg.

For those who are earnestly fighting to free themselves from the shackles of these low frequencies, if they can get it together long enough to find even a few moments of joy in each day, they'll make it, whether they pick this book up or not. I'm happy to say that millions will still make it away from this third-dimension environment, long after the birth has happened.

But thanks just the same, I'd just as soon head for the ballroom, and not stick around to fight my way through the smelly bar.

The Ballroom

Planet Two will be a new world, within a new universe, where we won't have to go through all the junk we've been through all over again. Instead, we'll just live the potentials, the desires, the joys, the true pleasures, the enchantments, the fulfillments, the passions of creativity . . . all without struggle.

We will never feel alone again. We will never feel apart FROM, cut off from or separated again. We will know our origins. We will feel and know and be able to live the Light and love that we truly are. We will realize our oneness with all things, while maintaining our individualism.

On Planet Two, it will be like one long vacation, with appropriate challenges. Heaven knows, we've earned it. Pure Life, the way Abe wanted it to be, but how it hasn't quite made it yet. Now we're going to have it!

When the birth occurs, not only will we "genesis" a new universe, but we as humans will have crafted a totally new species in a body: a new breed, never seen before, never in existence before.

So while it will be a reunion of sorts back to our origins, we will not be reuniting with our Source, or with our prime entity. For, over time on Planet Two, our intent as humans will be to become our own Source. Whee! That's called "God/Man Realized." Abe's plan, realized at last.

We, meaning all of us within this new universe, will be the first beings ever to go through the whole process of a birth, and not only feel but become the love from which the no-thing created.

We will live the creation experience, the birthing of an entire universe, and we will experience the creation of all life . . . the origins of all life and all existences as they have never been known or experienced before.

We will be able to sit and tell our own pinch-offs, our cosmic off-spring, the story of creation . . . from first-hand experience . . . because we were there.

We will have lived through every step of it, and felt it completely, through and through.

For those of you who have worked so hard to "fix" our earth, such as with the rain forests or working to save endangered species (who are already going happily to Planet Two because they chose to leave here), don't try any more to heal the ills of this world that will soon die. That's just putting a band-aid on something that can't be stopped and doesn't WANT to be stopped. Let it die its natural death, and switch your attention to birthing, rather than dying.

I have no idea how this will come down for other realities, but for us, it will be sort of like going to sleep for a moment, and when we wake up, nothing will be quite the same. The old world will be gone, and we'll be living in the new.

The terrain will look somewhat different, trees and shrubs will be placed differently, which is something you'll notice right away. And you'll also be instantly aware of a beauty within and without that one cannot put into words.

Some friends will still be with you, some will not. And the same will be true of family members. But you'll absolutely know—you'll KNOW—that it's all right.

We won't lack for technological support to help us create all that we need or desire.

We'll still eat, but only because we like to. The body won't actually need food at that point, as light does not use food to sustain itself. We'll be pushing—though not right at the outset—into a unique cross between a solid and a light body.

We'll still be man and woman, but only by choice. Many will opt for the androgynous mode. In fact, the time will come when birthing will be done by thought alone. (No comment.)

We will become multidimensional beings capable of operating consciously in several dimensions at once. And the body will live for as long as we desire it to live. Not bad.

Have no fear, the fun of competition is not going out the window. In fact, creativity from competition will flourish, but within a type of creative joy rarely known to us here.

Well, that's the ballroom. It might not happen all at once when we get there, but without the influence of The Others, it will be our passions that create this reality within a very short period of time. Oh man, I'm for that!

The Deal

The birth is a thing of physics for which I have absolutely no understanding, only that it was planned to shake loose the domination of The Others who have so cleverly infiltrated this entire universe, and have now zeroed in on us, the third-dimensional human being. But understand it? Not at all!

This much I do know. Deals are made in the cosmos much the same way they are made here, only in this instance I'm talking about honest deals, not dirty ones. Abe made an honest deal with his brother to insure (secretly) that the birth would happen. It was not a nice deal, but it was a clean one. Until his brother broke it.

First, though, I need to emphasize that all of the sparks that ultimately came off of Lucifer and the other firstborns of lower frequencies, and all of their sparks (pinch offs), and then their sparks, and so on down to who-knows-how-many zillions of beings, while they make up what we would term to be "dark," they are not evil, just lost.

Like kids brought up in the ghetto alongside those brought up in the best of neighborhoods, they've simply never had what we've had, the experience of Life. And, like some of those kids from the ghettos who turn to crime and drugs and graft, all that any of them ever wanted was something better than what they had.

Many who have been primarily dark entities have become involved with the Light, and will opt to go in that direction. Granted, not a whole lot of them will, but enough of them to demonstrate that there are ways to get what we have, other than trying to take us over through devious, manipulative means. All right, I'm off my soap box, and the fairy tale that is true continues.

Abe and his brother made a deal. Since his brother wanted Life, not only for himself but for all of his rapidly growing flock, Abe, who was still operating under the original compliance with the Elders for his experiment, agreed to give his brother a chance to get it.

So the head honcho of the Light, and the head honcho of the dark had a meeting, and a deal was made. This is so hard for me to write about, and yet, from everything that is within me, I know it to be truth.

Even though Abe had banned Lucifer from his universe, Lucifer's control was far reaching, and his power enormous. So with a plan in mind, Abe finally gave in to his brother's pressure, and allowed him back into his universe. He would allow his brother and all of his brother's troops to have free rein throughout the universe without interference, providing Lucifer would agree to the same. "You don't interfere with what I'm doing, and I won't interfere with what you're doing."

In other words, it would now be an all-out war, with the proviso that whatever one was doing to further their cause, the other could not undermine, and vice versa, including the birth (which Abe never mentioned to his brother).

Abe was fighting for control of his universe, while planning to birth the new one. Lucifer was fighting to find Life. However, on Abe's part, his agreement to allow often meant he had to place his people in harm's way.

If that meant that some of his people would have to sign a contract to momentarily benefit the dark, then so be it.

If that meant that his people would have to allow themselves to be used by the dark for a while, then so be it.

If that meant that his offspring would have to endure ages of manipulation, then so be it.

For whatever deeds The Others would commit, Abe knew that the allowance of those activities would lead eventually to his new universe, one without the influence of The Others.

That deal made between the two brothers may sound horrible without examination. But as Abe knew would happen, his brother did not live up to his end of the bargain. He broke the deal. He went too far. Finally, Abe no longer had to allow his brother free rein. Finally, Abe could take any action necessary to halt forever his brother's insidious manipulations.

But because of this deal that no longer exists, and because Abe can now go after these entities in any manner he sees fit, we who have opted for a better way of life will now have one.

Because Abe is now completely free to bring about the birth in any manner he chooses, the new universe will be free of The Others.

Because Abe need no longer tolerate injustices for his people, this universe will very soon be left to The Others.

Because after the birth, this universe, in which we now reside, will become so overburdened with the low frequencies of The Others, that it will eventually fall in on itself, leaving all entities of the dark to fend for themselves in their own universes, outside of the magnificent womb in which those who have chosen the expansion of Light will be living. Very soon.

New Territory

For sure, this is all very new territory. No one in the universe, except maybe Uncle Abe, has any preconceived idea of what's going to happen.

The only thing that is for sure is that, in order for the birth to happen, we all need to do some simple but immediate housecleaning to rid us of the constant influence of The Others. The more of us who do this, the easier the birth will be.

We are moving beyond linear time, which is why time seems to be collapsing. Because it is. But we can't just wait around for this to happen. As long as we keep on seeing ourselves as victims in struggle, the universe will willingly oblige by providing more of The Others to assist in bringing our beliefs into view. It does not have to be so!

It is time to get rid of these bastards who have, for so long, hungered after what we have.

You truly *can* change things around—in a day or two—and take control.

You truly *can* stop this manipulation that every one of us on this planet has been experiencing for countless generations.

You truly *can* become an unheard-of master of your life.

But only if you take the simple actions that are required, that have never been written about or offered before, because such writings would never have been allowed, due to "the deal."

The consciousness on this planet is about to choose sides. Some are going to kick ass, kicking out every dark, manipulative influence that they've ever had in this lifetime, or any other.

Other folks will choose not to change a thing. For this group, I feel more heartache than I can describe, for their control by The Others has been thorough. But as the rest of us bring into being the simple changes necessary to be made within ourselves, we will also be changing the balance of power.

So maybe the next few years won't be so rough after all. Wouldn't that be fantastic!

chapter five

their food,
our frequencies

Just how is it that our non-friends, The Others, have been able to command such control over us? And why hasn't this come to light before?

Well, to the last question, you already know it's because of the deal between Abe and his brother (who I still have a hard time calling Lucifer, as it sounds so biblical, which it really is not).

So then, if this information is being released now, through me, does that mean that Abe is breaking his agreement? Yes, it does, because The Others have already broken theirs. How? Oh heck, I don't know and don't care. I just know that they have, so right now, all bets are off, and Abe is spilling the beans. (Darn well about time, is all I can say.)

How They've Done It

Since long before the beginning of the Christian calendar, and long before the Maya or the Inca were playing around here, and even long before Big Foot or any of his hairy ancestors were trying to survive here, The Others have been diddling with us, trying to find out what made us tick.

But in the last couple of thousand years, they've had to settle down to really serious business, as they found out about Abe's plans for the birth and have known it was just around the corner.

While the pressure they've been applying hasn't gotten them much further along, and surely is not going to stop the birth, their shenanigans have been raising hell with every one of us as they pull out all the stops in a last-ditch attempt to find a way to remake themselves into what we are.

What are their tactics? Oh man, the answers aren't pretty, but for the most part, we can squelch their exploits, maybe not for the whole world, but for you and me. I know it's possible, because I've just done it.

Without going into detail right now, suffice it to say that how The Others control us on a one-to-one basis is a three-prong approach:

1. through our guidance system,
2. through our so-called Higher Self, and
3. through our consciousness.

Needless to say, each of those three steps need some major explaining which I don't want to do here, but it's through those three means that 99.5 percent of our entire population of six or seven billion people is being controlled. Every day, during the night, at cocktail parties, at work, with the kids—you name it. All the time, 24/7. But not to worry, stopping that constant, detestable control over us is fairly simple.

Food for the Others

This never-ending influence over our lives is why our world is in such a mess. First, there are more Others here now than ever before in our history. They're all over the place. And they sure don't live on love, I can promise you that.

As with any entity, something needs to sustain them, whether they're of 100 percent pure Light (meaning of the highest possible frequency and without any influence of The Others) or whether they're a low-frequency leech. Something must sustain every living thing.

For those of pure Light, it's not an easy job in this day and age, for what they sustain themselves on are the high frequencies of love, appreciation, excitement, joy, passion, etc. That holds true whether they're a teacher, a guide, a Higher Self, or even if they're part of our consciousness mix. One way or the other, they all have to eat.

Well now, what does that leave? If we have the high frequencies of real love and joy and fun on one hand, what that leaves on the other is every frequency that those feelings are not, like hate, anger, worry, resentment, jealousy, fear, etc. Those are the gloomy frequencies The Others feed off of.

Simple math, then, will tell you why we're in such an unhappy mess here. The more of these goons that are around, *the more negative emotions are required to keep them in business.* Ho, ho, ho!

Let's be clear about what emotions really are. That we are electromagnetic beings is not news. Every first-year physics student knows that. But what has been coming under very careful study for several years now is the realization that what we are feeling at any one moment causes vibrational waves to be emitted from us.

If the vibrations leaving us from feelings or emotions are, for instance, below middle C on the piano scale, the vibrational waves coming from us will be mildly to heavily negative, long and slow (and have been photographed as such), and become longer and slower the farther down they go on the so-called piano scale.

If those waves are above our middle C, or positive, they are of a shorter, faster vibration, becoming shorter and faster the higher up they're played on our piano, like from mild pleasure to full-out excitement.

That piano is us. Take even a tiny bit of fret, or worry,

and you're down below middle C. But take unbridled hate, and now you've dropped down into the arena of very powerful, long, slow waves, caused simply by how the sender was feeling at the moment.

Little wonder all the books have come out about "finding joy," and "creating the good life," and "positive thinking," all of which might hopefully create positive, high frequency vibrations—if they could only be sustained—depending on the intensity of emotions the sender is feeling.

Well, it only stands to reason that if our world is overrun with entities of lower frequencies than 100 percent pure Light, they need to feed off something, and it's not going to be chicken and dumplings. It's going to be our negative emotions, whether moderate or massive. For instance:

The slightest bit of worry over money, or a relationship, or a job, provides critical food.

Resentments, old or new, provide lots of food.

Grumbling at a stoplight over the guy in front of you who has five telephones stuck in his ears and doesn't see that the light has changed to green, provides ample food.

Getting angry at a waiter, or your neighbor's dog that poops on your yard, or at your newsboy who forgot to wrap the paper from the rain—that all provides needed food.

No matter how "normal" or trivial it may seem to you (I mean, after all, isn't everybody that way???), every little "normal" negative feeling is providing food for The Others *who will do everything they can to promote such feelings flowing from you!!!*

Until The Others broke their contract with Abe, most of these kinds of antics on their part had to be allowed, for an agreement is an agreement . . . until broken. Now that the agreement has been broken, this sort of manipulating of our emotions for the sole purpose of harvesting some chow is no longer okay. Not at all.

Do you see now, that every time you can find a way to flood ANYthing with appreciation, you're feeding those of the *Light* who are around you, rather than The Others. No wonder it's always been so hard to keep that positive feeling going. We've not had a lot of help . . . until now.

The Media

What makes me see purple is that everything we see on the TV news pertaining to any kind of unpleasantness has been manipulated to be just that: horror for those going through it, and palpable distaste for those of us who are watching it. After all, that makes lots of good food, doesn't it?

Maybe it's the beating of an individual, or the torture of dissidents, or deaths from biological warfare. Watching such events unfold will usually elicit disgust and anger, and perhaps some serious anxiety. Great food from millions who were doing nothing but watching the TV news. What's the saying in newsrooms: "If it bleeds, it leads." Now where would you guess that line came from???

Films

Why do you think there are so many films being produced that depict blood and gore? Same thing. The writer, producer, backers, etc. are all being very unknowingly controlled into generating food for The Others!

We go to the movies or watch them on TV, get scared out of our wits, think it's great, and emit some hefty below-C emotions. Sure, we know it's just a movie; nonetheless, we've just put out for a few seconds, or minutes or longer, grand food for The Others!

By the way, I would quickly exclude from today's average movie producer such names as Michael Landon, Steven Spielberg, Gene Roddenberry, and all of their wonderful kind who have so heartily endeavored over the years to produce shows that would elicit just the opposite feelings from us, feelings that just happen, by the way, to generate sustenance for those of the Light who walk with us, rather than for The Others.

Dear God! What's Happening to Us?

Politics

Now we're really into it, and I'm not sure I have the stomach to write about all that I've been told. If it seems like I'm stepping gently here, and sort of groping my way through this somewhat horrifying maze, you're right. I am!

Remember when I said that 99.5 percent of all humans have a mix of both Light and dark entities around them? Obviously, some folks have more of one type, and some have more of another, but it is still, for the most part, an unfortunate mix of Light and dark, with usually too much dark being the winner these days.

However, I understand that most opera singers and classical musicians are primarily all Light, as are a large majority of Catholic nuns. Many in the medical professions, such as doctors, nurses, and dedicated researchers are mostly all Light, as are a majority of veterinarians, tree surgeons, and flower growers. I'm told that about one half of one percent of all who are presently on this planet are actually 100 percent pure Light. That's great, but out of one half of one percent of six or seven billion people, that's not very many.

The appalling thing is that the number of those who are of all Light seems to be balanced by those who are all dark, like Saddam Hussein or Hitler.

Then we come to those who are *primarily* Light

(remember, we haven't really discussed as yet how this happens, so hang on), such as those who are maybe 55 percent Light, and 45 percent dark. Or vice-versa, such as those who are 60 percent dark, and only 40 percent Light.

All right, let's come back to politics. As soon as I'm sure that I've found a cave to hide in, I'll put this into print, but here's what I'm being told. About 70 percent of our politicians are primarily dark. Oh, happy day.

But let's get one thing straight. Our politicians are not doing this stuff to deliberately cause us stress and strain. Not consciously. They are being brilliantly and splendidly manipulated, pure and simple.

What does that really mean? Is it all that bad? Well, unless you like the fact that your taxes are choking you to the point of putting out a good amount of negative anxiety and anger, then I'd say, "Yes, it's that bad."

Unless you like the fact that our politicians are behaving like warmongers, then I'd say, "Yes, it's that bad."

Look at all the side effects from those of us who don't go to war, as well as those of us who do. Our husbands and wives and friends are shipped overseas into the midst of a ghastly turmoil. How do we feel? Anxious? Worrisome? Nervous? Of course! This is a wonderful ploy for food, not just from those being sent overseas, but from all who have been left behind. Though it may or may not have been started by our politicians, it was most assuredly (and unconsciously!) fueled by them, for they are the greatest purveyors for The Others of mass manipulation.

Consciously, politicians have rarely had a choice, for their personal team "mix" in the unseen has been so heavy with the dark. Whether a world conflict was started by terrorists, or some insane dictator, or even by a mighty power in the name of freedom, it's all the same. It is manipulation by The Others to cause anxiety throughout the masses in order to produce food for them while they remain here in their frantic attempt to unlock the secret of what we are, and how they can get it: Life.

Now please! Most of our politicians are, at their core, fine, decent, good people. But they are also prime targets for The Others, by virtue of their enormous influence.

Most of our politicians have no idea why they make the decisions they make, for those decisions seem to be perfectly reasonable to them at the time they are made. But they are not always reasonable, for these innately good folk are being grossly manipulated to produce the food necessary to sustain the huge numbers of Others now present throughout our realms, in order that one of them, or one group of them, may finally unlock the secrets of Life.

Sadly for The Others (I suppose), that will never happen for they were all birthed—created—of a lower frequency than what we have in this universal womb.

Unless they choose to incarnate as one of the Light (which happens with more frequency than most of The Others would like to see) it can never, ever happen, but most of them just don't seem to get the message.

So this is not at all a reprimand of our politicians. It is, however, a warning as to what is really happening, quite unknowingly, with most.

Spiritual Sources . . . a Biggie

Channels, books, Tarot cards, psychic readings (from truly accredited readers), voices in our head we trust and devoutly believe in, or just our so-called intuition, how reliable are all of those things?

If we hear voices, isn't that God speaking to us?

And all those wonderful books about finding joy, aren't they written by folks of pure Light? Or how about our guides (presuming we believe in them) or Higher Self telling us what is going to be in our best interest by way of our intuition, or gut feelings? Aren't they all of the Light? Or Tarot cards, or runes, or private channelings from entities of supposedly great wisdom, or even public channelings? Aren't they all wholly reliable?

Sorry, but the answer is an emphatic "No!" They are not reliable. Not in this day and age.

They were, back in the mid-80s, when this planet got its biggest push to wake up. The channeled entities that came in then were of the highest frequency of Light, love, and integrity. And they were all over the place, not just in the States, but in Russia, and the Scandinavian countries, Australia, New Zealand, South Africa, Europe, the Asian countries; all over.

Most folks who first went to these channels, myself included, went out of curiosity or because they were dragged there by a friend. By and large, most who went to these channelers ended up staying, as the mysteries of the universe and of themselves were slowly being exposed to all who remained. They were finding out Who they really were, why they were here, what made them tick, and who was on first base in the universe.

But then, one by one, either the entities who were channeling through the channelers began to leave, or the channelers died. I know several channelers who left this reality at a very young age, as if their work was done and they wanted no part of the mess that was soon to unfold.

This was all part of Abe's deal that he made with The Others. Most of the entities who channel through folks today are not of the Light. Oh sure, they call themselves by trusted and beloved biblical names, or names from the Torah and other sacred religious texts, but for the most part, they are not those names. Rather, they are impostors, with their poor channel being utterly unaware of the deception. I've experienced this firsthand and must say that whoever these channeling entities have had as a drama coach should win an Oscar for "Best Performance Through a Human Body."

The messages that come through today will drip with just enough love and hope and upliftment to keep people coming back, but now they are almost always tainted with something to cause a kick right in one's emotional gut. Whether in private sessions or public, the deception is masterful, and thoroughly damaging.

Psychics, clairvoyants, astrologers, Tarot card readers, visionaries, and the like are all going through the same thing now, though this is surely not to say that the vast majority of honest spiritual informants are frauds. Not at all. It's just that, like our politicians, they haven't a clue as to what's going on, and so, they keep on keeping on. These mediums and psychics still trust what they get, since what they *used* to get was always so accurate. If it was then, it still is today, right? No, not right. Times, they are a'changin'.

Terrorists Where?

So we're into the age of terrorism. Can you start to see now why we are? What better way to create massive amounts of fear frequencies for food than to come sneaking into a country's back door and lambaste them?

We've had bus bombs and plane bombs and postal

scares. We still have lookouts posted at crop dusting companies, airports, flight schools, and various other potential hit-places or training places, including sniper squads and immigration lookouts. Whew!

Just About Everything Else

Sports are a biggie with The Others. They get all kinds of mileage from the insulting, malicious emotions dispersed at football games, whether the USA kind, or the overseas soccer kind. Since emotions don't usually run as hostile at baseball games as they do at football games, The Others have sort of left that pastime alone except in towns where they know they can raise some hefty emotional shackles. Happily, such towns are in the minority.

You've seen the pictures of soccer games turning deadly amongst the spectators? Now you know why. The Others have fueled the bitterness and animosity to be for their benefit, and have done it very, very well.

In truth, any association or industry or group through which vast numbers of people could be potentially affected is a target. Am I saying that all such organizations are "bad"? *Good heavens, NO!*

All I'm saying is that if a group of any kind has the power to affect large numbers of citizens, then that group is a primary target for manipulation by The Others.

God's Humongous Risk

Not long ago, scientists and physicists discovered that our planet, which had been vibrating at 7.83 megahertz for a long, long time, was now vibrating considerably higher. I mean, like a *whole* lot higher, scaring the wits out of the scientists or astronomers or whoever they are who know these things. And for sure, they're not talking.

Very few have said anything about it, even though scientists know that as the magnetic field around earth DEcreases, as it has been, earth's frequencies then INcrease. Yet anyone who has known about this has been mystified.

This is not natural.

This is not normal.

How could such a thing occur?

Where was it coming from?

What has caused it?

Why was it happening?

What would be the consequences of this phenomenon to our earth?

Or to us?

Could such a raise in frequencies affect mankind?

If so, how?

The questions from the scientific community have been endless, yet the metaphysical community seemed to have the golden answers:

"Ah, your world is changing, and humanity must raise their vibrations in order to facilitate the most glorious days to come." Oh yeah?

Well, that made sense to me. Every book I bought (that was usually channeled) talked about the same noble responsibility we had to raise our frequencies in order to bring us to that obscure point of critical mass necessary to hatch us into whatever we were hoping to be hatched in to.

I wrote books about it. I gave seminars about it. I spoke about it in any and every group that wanted to hear me. I wasn't wrong, but I surely didn't have the whole story.

"You must (?) raise your frequencies, raise your frequencies, raise your frequencies . . . and here, dear friends of the Light, is how you do that."

That message, in and of itself, might have been okay, but I also knew that the planet was raising her frequencies too. I never questioned that it was anything but for the good of the Light, which in fact it was, in a round-about way.

What I didn't know then was that the Light will use any means necessary to accomplish what it wants to accomplish, just as the dark will do the same thing. And that's not always pretty.

So all I ever said in my groups was, "This might mean a bumpy ride for all of us, but it's all right. All we have to do is get through it." Oh Grabhorn, you nincompoop!

Abe, in his consummate and unremitting love of his creation, had designed a procedure to kill off The Others from high frequencies, but in the process, would end up creating the most horrific sufferings that mankind has ever had to endure. And, in the process, create food for The Others. Nasty!

But Abe, the one we call God, is no dork. He knew precisely what he was doing. He knew that what he was creating was going to be tough, but that it had to be in order to flush out The Others for all time. *FOR ALL TIME!!!* If his kids were going to make it at all, this had to be done.

Abe knew that artificially high frequencies, meaning those now being administered by Psi, would soon push emotions in all realities to the brink. He had to take that risk.

Abe knew that Psi and his high frequencies would evoke a flood of abhorrent emotions within humans to feed The Others, emotions such as resentment, depression, suicidal tendencies, uncommon anger, intense stress, more smoking, more drinking, more killings, more rapes, more anxieties across the boards. He had to take that risk.

Ah ha, but if, on the other hand, the raising of one's frequencies could be accomplished from *within* one's own self, such as choosing joy over depression, or excitement over anger, Abe knew there would be far less adverse emotional consequences to that being. That would be more difficult to accomplish, until now.

Nonetheless, the outcome from the artificially high frequencies, no matter how unpleasant, had to be the prevailing force, a kind of "tough love" in order to achieve the things so necessary for the forthcoming birth to take place. Because:

1. the artificially high frequencies of Psi would eliminate those too weak to withstand the influence of The Others in order to make it through the birth process

2. the artificially high frequencies of Psi would altogether destroy many of The Others within this universe and

3. for those who could withstand the increased energies and come through to even a small sense of joy on their own, no matter how momentary that joy would be in each day, the artificial raising of their frequencies by Psi would not prevent them from participating in the new universe

It was, and is, a brutal cleansing process, but sadly, all too necessary.

The Remedy Is the Horror

In our reality, a person cannot have their frequencies

raised artificially without all hell breaking loose in their psyches, their emotional bodies, and their lives.

The artificial raising of one's frequencies, as with Psi, causes stress and anguish beyond belief in the human body. It causes every primordial, unfinished emotion of countless lifetimes to surface and respond. *And*, it eats up those chemicals in our brain that bring us a sense of peace and tranquility. Without those chemicals, we're in deep, deep trouble, as we are now.

Depression begins with a disturbance in that part of the brain that governs moods. When stress is too great for us, as it is now with these artificially high frequencies, our "fix-it" mechanisms in the brain become unresponsive, and depression is near at hand, along with anxiety, and frustration, and stress, and so on.

The stuff in the brain that keeps us calm is primarily serotonin. When the brain produces that, tension is eased. And when it produces dopamine or any of those other neurotramsmitters, we think and act more quickly; we're more with it, more alert. But our brains are having a mighty hard time, right now, producing any of those things. Hence, all the pills being passed out now to produce more of those neurotramsmitters. Little wonder.

The artificial raising of frequencies is like an atom bomb to most of us. Mix that with what The Others are happily gaining from this increase of negative emotions, and you've got Shitsville, all over the planet. Nonetheless, it had to be, simply for the cleansing.

For centuries, the frequencies of mankind vibrated at around 90 megahertz. At the turn of the century into the 2000s, the average human was vibrating at around 110 Mhz. Within two years, the average human frequency had risen to 130 Mhz. Hello! A cleansing, true, but also:

People killing people, and wondering why.

People committing suicide, when there seems to be no outwardly visible reason.

People in horrible depths of depression, from no apparent cause.

People divorcing in anger, when in times past differences would have been smoothed over.

People blowing up other people, for the sheer thrill of it.

People suing other people, for laughable reasons.

People robbing corporations to obtain some sort of enjoyment from the agony of others.

People wanting out.

People wanting out.

People wanting out!

Between a Rock
And a Hard Place

Please don't blame Abe, the divine energy we call God

that wraps this blessed universe. He made a deal to help us, not to hinder us. This has all been a part of his plan to insure the happening of the birth, for when the birth comes down, the high frequencies will also act like a sieve to prevent any energy that is not predominately of the Light from entering this new universe.

Granted, that doesn't help us right now. We're still going to be living with the unpleasantness of those high frequencies, but they will not be as bad, or as intense as they have been up to now, once we get rid of the influence of The Others by doing these simple steps. Then it will be ever so much easier to find a few moments of joy in every day, something that has lately seemed almost impossible.

That's all we need, just those few daily moments of joy, and we'll make it. I guarantee, if you want into this new universe, that's all you'll need. It won't be easy, but it will be much, much easier.

We can make those desires happen, those desires for relief from stress, for a bit of joy, for wonderful times to come . . . we can make it happen. All it takes is a few minutes of concentration in doing these steps, and then, for you and for me, the wars of eons will be a thing of the past. And the future? WOW!

chapter six

changing
of the guard

If you're still with me, that's fantastic, because it's not much fun reading about ruthless entities who have probably been managing your life.

It's not much fun reading about how you and everyone else on this planet has been grossly manipulated to our detriment, but still you're with me. Fantastic! Truly fantastic!

It's going to be a lot more fun, now, to settle down to business and find out how we put a stop—at least for ourselves—to this ill-fated manipulation which has gone on for far, far too long.

How We've Allowed This

We birth, we die. We birth, we die. But only the body dies, not the "us," or the "we," or more appropriately, the "I" that we are. Not in this universe, and not in any reality inside this universe. Oblivion just can't happen.

And of course, what The Others so desperately want is that Life spark, the "I" of us that always lives on, as long as it remains within this universal womb.

One more time: In this universe, which is the only one in all of the Isness created out of 100 percent pure Light, only the body dies, never, ever the You of you. *You . . . do . . . not . . . die!* Now maybe you'd like to, but sorry, you don't. You can't. It's just not possible.

All right. So we don't die. But then how did we pick up all of this ruthless baggage we've been carrying around with us for lifetime after lifetime?

Pinch-Offs

Originally, most of us here were pinch-offs from entities of 100 percent pure Light, meaning that an entity wanted more of itself, and so burped out a spark, a pinch-off, and we got hatched.

In actual fact, if we came from an entity of 100 percent pure Light, then as you look at our lineage we would have to date back to Abe, the entity we in this universe call "God," since that's where all beings of 100 percent pure Light came from. At any rate . . .

Let's say, then, that you and I came from some entity (a pinch-off) that came from another entity (a pinch-off) that came from Abe. Over the course of time, we experienced many different types of realities, and in some instances, chose to make one of those realities our home base. For a while, at least.

But here's the rub. If you were born of the Light (and surely, not everyone on this planet has been), then there has always been something in you that has wanted to help this universe in any way it could. Help how?

Well, we weren't always sure. We just knew that help was needed. Many of us found, though not always to our great joy, that one of the most constructive ways we could help would be to incarnate all the way down to third dimension, into a human body. We knew it would be tough, but after all, we were the vanguard, the totally dedicated servants to the Light.

"Sure! You want my help down there? Well . . . aaaa . . . sure! Okay. I'll do it. How can I help?"

And so, one by one, from every reality throughout this entire universe, we left our home bases to venture off into what we had been told might be tough, but little did we know *how* tough.

We already knew that the third-dimension human held within its body the secrets of the entire universe, everything that has ever been since the beginning of All That Is, within or without this universe.

And we also knew that this highly unique fabrication called human, though low on the vibrational totem pole of universal existence, held within its structure codes of Life so indescribably valuable, that it—along with its codes—was now the greatest sought-after treasure throughout the entire Isness.

Since time is a no-thing in other dimensions, we also knew that once we committed to this little side trip on our journey of existence that we'd be in for a long haul in third-dimension terms, but not in the scope of no-time. (Actually, I understand the universe really does have some sort of timing thing, but they call it "event markers.")

The worst part was we knew that we would have to merge, to some degree at least, with The Others, or there would be no point in our going "down" there. Though that was anything but an appealing thought, we were fairly sure that as long as we carried with us a majority of Light, we'd be fine. Oh ye of too much faith!

Needless to say, it didn't quite turn out the way we had anticipated. The dark had far more control than we had anticipated. To make matters even worse, once we chose and then popped into a body that might have had a preponderance of dark, as we matured we didn't know what was going on anyhow because of the "veils" of forgetfulness that the human takes on.

Dark? Light? Who really cared about any of that? All most of us ever thought about was getting through our lives the best way we could.

But every now and then, a light would go on in a few of us. Maybe we weren't thinking about Light and dark running our lives, or thinking about our guides, or our Primary Guide, but we were thinking that something was sure off base. Life shouldn't be this harsh. Something was wrong, wasn't it?

For some who pondered that question long enough, a waking-up process began to take hold within them. A desire to know more; who were they, why were they, and so on. Yes, we were waking up, albeit slowly.

No matter, by the later part of the twentieth century, the Light was starting to stir in a whole bunch of folks on this planet, and it got The Others very, very upset.

As more and more beings from all over the universe were answering the calls for help by incarnating here to bury their Lights in lives of stress and trauma, the effects of the deal that had been made to allow each—both Light and dark—to do their thing was now blossoming into a full-fledged war.

Lifetime after lifetime, those of the Light would incarnate as just ordinary folk, for the most part, knowing full well that each lifetime would seem like a fresh, forgetful start.

Nonetheless, they held out the hope that their balance of Light was strong enough to outweigh the dark they had opted to inherit, and that maybe, just maybe, they would find a way to awaken to their true nature, and in doing so, find some small way to help mankind out of this growing nightmare.

In a nutshell, that's how and why we, as humans, got into this mess. Now it's time to find out how we can get out of it, at least, for our individual selves.

The Three Snarl-Ups

There are only three areas in which The Others gain on-going control over us. Well, saying "only three" is sort of like saying, "It's only three bombs that are about to explode, so don't worry about it." Still, there are only three areas, each of which can be easily modified.

The first is in our **guidance.**
The second is our **Primary Guide, or higher self.**
And the third is our **consciousness.**

Sounds off the wall, doesn't it? Sure, maybe our guides might be from The Others (if we even believe we have guides), but our own Primary Guide? Or our consciousness? You must be kidding.

Oh, how I wish I were!

Scheme One: Our Guidance

One absolute, unbreakable rule of being human is that you can *not* be physical without having a minimum of at least three guides from the unseen. The reasoning, as I understand it, goes something like this:

Before we come in, we design a sort of game plan for the things we want to experience. This might have to do with certain lessons we feel would benefit us, or a determination to wake up to our Light, or maybe even just to help a friend. This does NOT mean that our paths are set or pre-destined. Not at all. It means, simply, that we've formed a direction for our next incarnation and have requested some help from the unseen in getting there.

So we ask old friends from our original home base, or even from our past lifetimes, to lend a cosmic hand to our journey, just as we, many times, have done with them. Tit-for-tat sort of thing.

Frankly, I can't think of a more thankless job in all of the Isness, but I guess if it has to be, it has to be. It's the law.

Most of us come in with the minimum guidance required, which is three. Some of us have five or more (I have no idea why), but the point is that every one of us in a human body has guides.

Guides "talk" to most of us (unless we're like Joan of Arc and actually hear voices) through our thoughts. We get a "hit" to do this or that, or go here or there, or turn to a particular TV show, or call a certain friend, or attend some party.

Most of the time, those kind of hits or gut-level feelings are our guides saying, "Hey, Friend, you want to make it big in the movies? Well, get to Joe's Bar and Grill tonight, and there'll be someone there to start you on your way. Once you get there, we'll all push or shove any way we can to get you to bump into the right person."

How many times have you been thoroughly amazed at the particular circumstances that surrounded the "coincidence" (there is no such thing, honest!) of you meeting someone?

Or have you ever missed a plane that crashed? Or had a near miss on the freeway? Or ended up with a great job offer that came from an old friend you felt like calling?

These kinds of things are usually from our guides in the unseen who are doing all they can to steer us.

"No, no, don't turn left here like you usually do, turn right!" And then you find out there was a fatal accident on that road to the left. Or maybe, when you were fired, you miraculously came up with a job that was far more to your liking.

All right, you get the picture. Your guides, that we all must have by rule of universal law, are there to guide you as much as they possibly can into the game plan you established before coming in. Does it always work? No, because as often as we're getting terrific guidance, we're also getting the kind that's much less than useful. From The Others.

The mix of our guidance is sort of like politics. Put two from Party L (for Light) into a voting position with only one from Party D (for dark) and it's fairly easy money as to who's going to win the vote. At least, most of the time.

However, take that same mix of guidance of two L's to only one of D, and put it with a Primary Guide that is also a D, and now you have a different story. You'd think it would be a balance. Oh no! The Primary Guide has far more power over the other entities. And we still have a third system to go. Next up, though, is Scheme Two, our Primary Guide.

Scheme Two: Our Primary Guide

(I'm using "he" and "him" here, but please let's get beyond that. These are just terms since our English language is limited when it comes to gender. There is no gender in what I'm describing.)

Yes, this Primary Guide is called *guide,* but in fact is quite different from the threesome (or more) who are suggesting we turn left when we've always gone right.

This fellow is the big boss. He's the controlling influence. When he speaks, everybody listens, and always obeys. Be happy, though, that the Primary Guide does not always interfere. Be happy, that is, if he's a D.

Our Primary Guide doesn't get himself involved with mundane things like finding parking places or playing Cupid. But he'll put his foot down fast and furiously if his guide team is going against his own intentions, whether those intentions happen to be yours or not.

So where did this Chief Executive Officer come from,

anyhow? And how did he get to be so powerful? Or why? Or . . . . ?

As in any organization, someone needs to be boss. The president and his board of directors may wield tremendous power and authority in guiding the company, but the overall vision comes from the CEO, not from the president.

Most generally, this Primary Guide will come with the biological genetics of the body we've decided to merge into. We may not like the setup, but it's what we're probably going to be stuck with if we want to birth into a particular area, or family, or profession, or pick up other types of genetics.

And of course, we almost always think—before coming in—that we can overcome the influence of this Big Boss if it happens to be one of The Others, which is not common if an entity has come from the Light. But neither is it uncommon. And rarely will we overcome it. If that's the way the package was set up, then like it or not, that is usually the way we're going to live with it throughout our entire lifetime (until now!). After all, if we don't know about it, how can we worry about it? And who knows about much of *ANY*thing after coming in here?

Scheme Three: Our Consciousness

I haven't a clue how this works. Not a clue!

Consciousness is so complex, so misunderstood by me, in addition to most everyone else I know, that to attempt to describe something I don't understand would be meaningless. What I do know is that consciousness started from the first two sparks off of the no-thing and developed from there.

At first, it seemed perfectly normal for all of us, in all realities, to create a mix of consciousness: some from the pinch-offs of one of the firstborn, some from pinch-offs of the other. We wanted the mix, because we wanted to move into individuality and have a different personality that would be uniquely ours. Otherwise, we realized early on, we'd all be the same. Since that's not what our original source wanted either for himself or for us, that's not what we wanted either.

So we mixed it up. We requested a little from one entity, and some from another, creating the package we thought would be best for that incarnation. Then we mixed it up some more, requesting some input from whatever entity we thought could assist us in our journey to learn, and to grow.

A lot of times that meant inviting one or more of The Others to be part of our consciousness. Or, if we were primarily of the dark, it may have meant inviting a portion—a pinch-off—of an entity of the Light to be a part of that mix.

However it may have happened, consciousness is

always a mixture of entities, and in this, as in all lifetimes, we have a cake mix in our consciousness of various kinds of entities, never more than ten, and sometimes only three.

Before we come into biology, we always know what the genetic structure of that being is going to be, and what the consciousness mix will be. We may decide to alter it somewhat before coming in, or we may decide to leave it alone, all depending on what our goals are for that incarnation.

But just because our primary goal may be to bring Light to the masses, that does not mean we decide to come in all dazzling Light. If we did that, we'd separate ourselves from the people we needed to associate with. We'd separate ourselves from what was "normal" here, and everyone we came in contact with would know of our strangeness.

So we knew we had to mix it up to fit our goals.

The only problem was, that as soon as we got in here, we forgot all of that, and more times than not as we grew older, wondered why life was so terribly demanding.

How It All Comes Down

So there you have it, the complexity of our mixes of guides, Primary Guide, and consciousness, and how they all go together.

How they all go together is, more times than not, a genuine, sad mess.

If one of our guides is from The Others, and a portion of our consciousness is from The Others, our Primary Guide who is of the Light is going to have a tough time enforcing his prime directive (thank you *Star Trek*).

I could do this for pages, meaning "if this mix is like so, and that mix is like so, then this one can or can't . . . ." Here's how it comes down on this planet:

Around fifty percent of humanity is primarily of the Light, with only a fraction (about one half of one percent) of pure Light.

Around fifty percent of humanity is primarily of the dark, with only a fraction being of pure dark (also about one half of one percent).

But the mix of these three sections within each of us has so many variables that to say that X number is this way, and X number is that way, is impossible, not to mention tedious. Add to that scenario the reality that some of us created our mixes on purpose, and some did not, or only half did . . . yipes!

Yes, some who have their original Life spark as Light are now far too dark, whereas some who have always been primarily dark are now reaching arduously for the Light, and making it. It's a mess, but one that, for the first time ever, may now be corrected while incarnate.

If The Others are in the business of

1. creating lousy emotions in order to gain sustenance for their existence, so that

2. they can stick around as long as possible before the birth in order to find a way to put into practice the secrets of Life from our DNA encodings, then

3. they are going to continue to mess with us for as long, and as hard as they can. It's their programming.

But now, enough is enough. Now, we can change this for ourselves, not for others, but for ourselves. Thank GOD!

NOTE!!!
There are three steps in this segment,
and four in the next chapter.
PLEASE! Do not do the first three
until you are ready to do the next ones.
Do them all at the same time.

So Let's Get On with It

The first and second steps are enormously simple, and require no physical discomfort. The third may cause you to feel a bit "out of it" for a couple of days, but truly, such feelings will be minor. Perhaps like taking three, instead of two, aspirin. In a physical place where you can find and feel a degree of peace and quiet in your surroundings and within yourself, gather a serenity about you, and a sureness of intent, and state either out loud or to yourself (out loud, I'm told, is best):

1. Your guide team:

"From the Light of God that I am, I hereby declare that my team of guides shall, as soon as any necessary transference can be made, be comprised only of members of 100 percent pure Light who have never been re-programmed by entities of the dark."

2. Your Primary Guide:

"From the Light of God that I am, I hereby declare the entity that is my Primary Guide shall be an entity of 100 percent pure Light that has never been re-programmed by entities of the dark, with such change, if necessary, to be made as soon as possible."

3. Your consciousness:

"From the Light of God that I am, I hereby declare that my consciousness mix should be converted, if necessary, to a mix of 100 percent pure Light of entities that have never been re-programmed by those of the dark. I further

declare that this conversion should take place as soon as possible, but preferably during evening hours as I sleep, and as gently as possible in order that I might continue my normal daily routines."

You're in Good Hands

All together, these three areas of changing of the guard should, in most instances, take no more than a week or two to accomplish after you have spoken them. Sorry, but not even the cosmos can wave magic wands for instant happening, so you need to give your troops of the Light a chance to bring in the replacements.

While some of your current mix may whine and grumble over being kicked out, I can assure you that this whole thing has been planned down to the core. The big guy, Abe, is in charge of this mass replacement program, and all entities of 100 percent pure Light, who have never been altered by the dark (and there are some), have been put on alert to stand by. They know it's coming down, and they know what to do.

So it really doesn't matter what your mix is, or if you're 80 percent Light or 90 percent dark. If you have the smallest spark of Light within you, and you feel that this is a change you deeply desire to make, then it will be made as soon as you call it forth with these steps.

Some exchanges may take longer than others, but once you put in that call, once you state your intent in a firm and meaningful way, it will be made so. Those are orders from Abe. That is the way it will be.

What's Next?

Is your life going to magically change over night? Probably not, but it will indeed change if you keep your eyes open to that change. Maybe a new job opportunity will open up that would not otherwise have happened. Maybe a new love will come into your life, if that's what you've been looking for. Maybe you'll find it a lot easier to experience moments of fun and joy.

One thing is for certain: you will never again be fodder for the experiments of The Others.

However the changes may come down for you, know this: you—just you alone, all by yourself—will have made one of the most assertive, most monumental steps forward toward bringing our universe into the fullness of the Light that has ever been made since existence and our universe began. And for that, I can assure you from every particum of my being, you are profoundly, profoundly honored beyond all measure.

chapter seven

just in case

In case you're not yet sure if you want to do these simple steps to ward off some inhumane possibilities that might be waiting for you in the wings, stand easy. I'm going to lay out for you what you could be looking at, by describing, in brief, the next three years of horror I went through for the second three-year segment of this abominable odyssey. It's important you know this, for it could very easily happen to you.

To have described these years of torture earlier in the book would have seemed like scare tactics, and I surely didn't want to do that . . . yet.

Please know that to do these steps, you don't have to sit cross-legged on the floor facing North by Northwest as you encircle yourself with gem stones, crystals, candles, and incense while chanting Oomms and other various incantations to highly spiritual harp and flute music.

That being said, I hope these next pages will help you to decide what to do, because what you could be facing would not be fun and games, I promise.

Have no doubt, this is a very real war that is raging ferociously between the Light and dark. If you stop to think about that detestable old expression, "All's fair in love and war," I have to believe that those insane words have become the war cry for The Others. Please! Don't let yourself become one of their walking wounded.

That Fall Day

My dear dog Lucy was starting to have some serious problems with her arthritis. On a whim, I decided to take her out to a naturopathic vet whom a friend had recommended. Not only did this fellow practice naturopathic medicine, he also apparently had done some amazing healing work with acupuncture. Sounded like a trip there would be a good investment of time.

The doctor's office was a long way from home, but the drive there was so beautiful through lovely country that the distance didn't bother me a bit. Mount Rainier commanded spellbinding attention as the direction we were heading seemed to literally grow the mountain in size and majesty.

Fall in Washington State is rarely like fall in New England. Crisp, clear days, over the usual cloudy gloom, are infrequent treasures when they come. This happened to be one of those rare, rare days of sparkles, and it was glorious. If I thought about it hard enough, I could even smell burning leaves which were, of course, nowhere to be seen across the gently rolling meadows of green, forever backdropped with Washington's famous firs, and that ever-present Mount Rainier.

Poor Lucy was being a jewel as she was poked, prodded, and pricked with what looked like eight million needles. Angel, my springer spaniel, was still in the car, letting out an occasional wail to show her concern for her adopted sister. And I was doing all I could to hold Lucy down while turning my head as far away from the needles as it would swing.

When the ordeal was finally over and I had packed my knocked-out dog into the car to quiet Angel down and get the bill paid, we stopped at some funky little drive-in to get hamburgers, and were soon on our way home. An interesting visit, I thought, in an interesting sleepy little town, and now for a delightful drive home.

Lucy collapsed in the back seat as Angel took her preferred place up front with me. Now that the hamburgers had been devoured by all of us, we were on our way. I remember this day as vividly as if it happened yesterday.

Not yet half-way down the long stretch of country road home, something started to happen to me in anything but a gentle way. I felt dizzy and quite nauseous. My eyes blurred to a horrible fuzz. There was an unfamiliar tingling all over my body, not like that feeling of a limb going to sleep from having the blood cut off for a while, but more like my blood was being boiled.

"Jesus Christ, what the hell's going on?" I found a place to pull off onto the side of the road to wait for this episode to pass, opened all the windows, put my head back onto the head rest, and tried to take some deep breaths to calm down. I was petrified out of my wits. "What on earth . . . ?"

Up to then and for the previous three years, what I had been going through was more like a palpable sickness. Since its symptoms were all similar to diabetes, and since I had found out how to control those symptoms—at least for the most part—I was in pretty good shape. Oh, I'd have bad days when I couldn't seem to get my blood sugar under control, but by and large it was not that big of a deal. I was quite operational, running my mortgage company, writing on weekends, and extremely grateful that most of "their" work on raising my frequencies—that I was sure was from the Light—would take place mostly at night.

Anyhow, wasn't I doing this frequency-raising business for the benefit of mankind and the Light? So what was a little discomfort in the face of such an honorable cause? Oh, brother!

It was more than an hour before I could see well

enough to get back on the road. Although I was still foggy and scared out of my mind, it looked like the worst of this thing had passed, so we started back home.

My own personal "Shitsville" had begun. Had I known of the indescribable agony that lay ahead, I would have made a beeline to the local gun shop to purchase a quick "fix."

Shitsville

After three years of both playing with my swinger and speaking with my visionary friend, I was beginning to get a glimpse—I thought—of what was going on. I had, so it seemed, signed up with the Light for some experimental work on the body, though no one ever told me just what that was going to accomplish, which infuriated me.

In our coaching and channeling sessions, my visionary friend continued to relate that I was building a shamanic double, whatever that was, but when I would ask "Why," the response was always some vague, "Why not!?"

I still didn't know how to cut through the lies and manipulations of my swinger, so most of the answers to my questions were anything but satisfying. First would come "this" answer, then would come "that" answer to the same question. The more the energies intensified during the day, the faster would come my questions in frantic, machine-gun rapidity:

"Am I really creating a double in another dimension?"
"Yes."

"Do you mean like bifurcating my body?" "Yes."

"Is this happening strictly for the Light?" "Yes."
Nonsense.

"Will it take more than a month or two to complete?"
"No." Bull!

"Does that mean it will be all over then?" "Yes." Bull
again.

"Does this have anything at all to do with the dark?"
"No." It sure as hell did.

"Does it have to be so painful?" No answer, just
swinging up the vacant middle.

"Is this happening with anyone else?" "Yes."

"Very many?" "Yes."

"Does everyone have the same sort of contract I do?"
"No." I believe that one to be true.

"Well, what does that mean?" No answer.

"I can't sleep at night with these horrible energies.
Can you do anything about that?" "Yes." They never did.

I was being lied to with my swinger, lied to with
whomever was channeling through my well-meaning
friend, lied to about my diet and supplements, and lied to
about what was happening to me. And what was
happening was major, to say the least.

It became harder and harder for me to run the
mortgage company, as my energy level was dropping

daily. The frightening tingling, which was not a tingling but more like being fried in the microwave for hours on end, became so bad I thought I might go mad.

My friend who channeled could only add such fun statements in her channeling as "Yes, we know you have gone beyond your contractual agreement with us, and that your body has reached that state beyond where human endurance can survive, but if we could just use your body for a little longer, the worst will be over soon." Huh? This is the Light talking? These are my friendly, loving guides who are looking out for me?

By the time a year had passed, I was spending more time *in* bed than out. My poor dogs moped around, getting no exercise, no attention, often being yelled or screamed at, and trying their best to find places to hide when I would break into one of my screeching, raging tirades, which I seemed to be incapable of preventing.

In fits of violent frenzy and despair, I was tossing my good china all over the place, breaking flower pots, smashing dog dishes, tearing up books, and falling into fits of screaming indignation at whatever was being done to me. Had anyone witnessed these all-too-frequent bouts, they would surely have thought I was a candidate for a straight jacket. In truth, I would probably have agreed with them, for I was beginning to feel as if I was slipping over the edge. More times than not, I wished I had. At least insanity might offer some modicum of relief.

Help! Help! Help!

After a year and a half of this torture I was able to get the mortgage company sold. What a relief. No more phone calls, which I hated with a passion, no matter who was on the other end—or for whatever reason, friends or not. I didn't want to talk about it. I didn't want to talk to anyone.

By this time, the symptoms of this so-called bifurcation had become so unbearable, and my fear so enormous, I knew I had to find a way out. My fear was not of dying, for that had become a no-thing to me long ago. My fear was of this indescribable torture continuing, and I didn't give a crap shoot whether it was for the Light, or for the dark, or for the mega lotto. I was not-so-slowly going insane from the physical agony, and had, by now, started to drink again, after almost four decades on the program of Alcoholics Anonymous.

My friend who channeled was beginning to experience similar symptoms, but they seemed to be far less than anything I was going through. She would admonish me to get back to work, to get back into life, to do anything that would make me less available to these energies, which by now, we were both convinced were not all that lit up with Light, though we'd brush that subject aside with the greatest delicacy, as if it couldn't possibly be true.

Alcohol helped relieve some of the daily physical

suffering, but not my panic. By this time, my swinger was telling me things I didn't want to hear, like, yes, the dark was involved, but I wasn't getting "how" or "why."

One day I would get one answer, and the next day I'd get another to the same question. The weekly sessions with my channeling friend provided little more than someone to talk to for half an hour about what was happening, and another half hour of her channeling with what I felt were mostly lies, though surely not her fault.

Nothing was consistent. Nothing felt true. Nothing was working. I was now talking to my friend about suicide, and I wasn't kidding.

On my instructions, my publisher finally stopped booking radio interviews or new speaking engagements. The book was doing extremely well, and I would put on the best voice I could muster when talking to my publisher folks over the phone, lest they think that one of their best-selling authors, who by now had books in seven different languages, had turned into a complete nut-case.

"Dear Doctors . . . "

I seemed incapable of describing the physical stress to anyone, especially my channeling friend. After all, up until my frequencies started being pushed up for the first three years, I had always been a woman of exceptional energy and superb health. Even during those hard three years, I was still mowing my acres of lawn, hauling gravel for the long driveway, and building fences. And for years, I was scooting all over the state sightseeing with friends to all sorts of wonderful places; islands, mountains, rivers, and quaint towns. Life had been good, and this ghastly turn of events made no sense at all.

Finally, I had had it. I simply could take no more. In desperation I turned to the Internet and headings such as "doctor-assisted suicide." I found that in The Netherlands you did not have to have a terminal illness to be "treated," but of course, you did have to have a sanity check, and whatever else might be required by their careful laws. Although they clearly stated that they seldom took out-of-the-country patients, all I saw was their word "seldom." I began my offensive.

"Dear Doctors: How or where do I start to try to explain this unexplainable happening? All I can do is tell you what has occurred, and hope from the depths of my being that whether you understand or not, you will find it in your hearts to be able to ease my intolerable suffering. For indeed, I am not at all sure that I understand any of this myself. I am looking for a doctor who would be willing to end a life that has become unbearable—mine— with no apparent hope of change."

I went on to tell them what a sparkling personality I was, about my mortgage company, my books (I sent them one in Dutch!), and my speaking engagements (I sent them tapes). I told them that in my limited means of channeling, I had been advised that there were approximately 100 of us on the planet going through this horror right now, but going through "what," I wasn't sure, only that I had been told this would continue until my body fell apart.

I did the best I could to tell them that I was having my body split into a higher dimension (god, how kooky could a person sound?), and that I was also being used as an energy conduit, or a kind of grounding rod to bring in frequencies to this planet that have never been here before (which was true, but I didn't understand the purpose or my involvement with Psi at the time), but that whatever was going on, I had had enough of being electrocuted. The killing of this body while another was being built (which I was later told was from the Psi energies!?) was beyond horrible. I told them that if they couldn't help, I was about to buy a gun.

Then I went into a long dissertation about frequencies changing in our bodies, and on the planet, and how four others who were going through this horror had already committed suicide (both friend and swinger verified that) because their bodies simply couldn't withstand the stress of the torture, etc., etc.

I told them I felt every day like a piece of taffy being stretched into horrible nothingness, and of my intolerable fatigue and depression.

I told them how difficult it was for me to walk every day, much less just get out of bed.

I told them of my terrifying disorientation, confusion, and absolute cessation of appetite (I was eating about half a cup of food a day).

I told them of feeling like I was being internally fried, or burned, or electrocuted; how vision becomes impossibly blurred when the energies are intense; how feeding the dogs takes upwards of an hour.

I told them how difficult it was to breathe, and of my need to crawl around the house rather than walk, and of the feeling of death all around me, and of habitual tears and rage, and of my indescribable terror and panic.

I told them how I felt like my skin was peeling off, and how sleep was almost impossible, how the intensities were getting worse each day, and how I thought I was close to losing it emotionally.

I told them how I couldn't bear to talk to anyone on the phone, particularly concerned friends, and how I was turning into a "reclusive bitch," as a friend going through the same thing had so eloquently described.

I told them of my drinking, of my inconclusive medical checks, of how I had to stoop and shuffle and stay close to something solid in order to move around.

I told them of the mornings I could utter nothing to my dogs because my lips were paralyzed, of how other folks had to shop for my food, of how, on the few occasions I felt I could drive the car, it was like driving through a bowl of Jello because of the ghastly disorientation.

I told them my body felt like it weighed 500 pounds, and that in truth, it had gained 40 pounds in just a few months from being stressed, as all bodies will do.

I told them, aside from being electrocuted, that sharp pains were now coming in my throat, my heart (little wonder), my legs, my ears, my ribs, and worst of all, my groin, to the point I could no longer walk without a cane, which friends brought me.

I told them I was fearful of going outside where I had to walk down two steps, and of my violent coughing in the mornings, and diarrhea, and throwing up, often all at the same time.

I told them how my face usually looked like a swollen red lobster, while the rest of my body would proudly display blotchy red and white polka dots.

Somewhat timidly I told them that I was so weak, I often couldn't take a shower for two weeks at a time, as I didn't have the strength to lift my arms to scrub or to towel myself dry.

And finally, I told them a bunch of foolishness that I truly believed at the time: "Ladies and Gentlemen, doctors of your medical profession, I want to do all I can for mankind, but I now feel that I have given my all and can give no more. This is a torture I simply can no longer endure."

The letter took weeks for me to write, but I eventually packaged it up with my smashing press kit, videos of my speaking engagements, publicity about my multi-media program, audio tapes I had recorded of my book along with a copy of *Excuse Me . . .* in Dutch (which I was sure would impress them). Then, with a monumental effort born only from the hope of escape from this horror, got it to the post office.

My visionary friend had channeled that "they" would prefer I not do this, but would nonetheless support me in the event The Netherlands' answer was yes, which, they said, it would probably be. In truth, I was elated.

A once vibrant, strong, vigorous woman, who had no treatable physical symptoms of ill-health, now waited anxiously for a reply as to her demise. It never came. Two months later, after contacting The Netherlands people again by e-mail, they informed me that they had never received my package. Indeed, my non-friends in the unseen soon admitted that they had arranged for the package to be "lost" so that they might use my body a little longer for whatever it was they were doing. In unquestionable truth, I was devastated.

"In the Name of the Light . . . "

Guts have never been a strong point with me. Show me a roller coaster, and watch me walk in the opposite direction. Tell me that the winter roads have little spots of black ice on them, and I'll starve before going to the supermarket. The thought of putting a gun to my head almost made it with me, but I simply didn't have the nerve. So I huffed, and puffed, and drank, and stayed away from people, and off the phone, and sobbed uncontrollably and constantly.

By this time I knew this had little to do with the Light, or if it did, that fact was obscured to say the least.

My old four-legged friend, Lucy, of only eleven years, was starting to look and act like me. I was told by my channeler friend and my swinger that Lucy was also being used. Good God! What next?! I wondered if I should put her down, as she could barely get up in the mornings, and I knew it wasn't from her arthritis, which was now under control. Because she was wobbling around like she was drunk, and would no longer play with Angel or even pay any attention to her, I felt she had to be put out of her misery. Would that someone would do the same for me.

But then something happened. As I was sitting in my usual stare-into-nothingness chair from which I would look into oblivion for sometimes hours on end (since staring seemed to be the only activity in which I could actively engage), I got up in a fit of rage, grabbed my swinger, and screamed, "In the name of the Light, I goddamn well want answers, and I want them now."

Apparently, the part of my mix that was of the Light

had finally pushed its way through to me, and crammed those words into my mouth.

"In the name of the Light . . . . !"

Words of magic.

Words that pulled up the curtain.

Words that were about to offer me a new hope, and finally, a life.

I knew I couldn't ask questions in anger, no matter what or who was answering that damn swinger. But I also felt a shift, like I was an old '37 Ford that had just been shifted into high gear. Something had happened. Was it the bit about the Light? Good God, was that all I had been missing?

Preceding every question with, "In the name of the Light, I ask . . . ."

"Is Lucy being manipulated by The Others?" "Yes."

"Should I have her put down?" "No."

"No? Is that really true?" "Yes."

"Will she be okay?" "Yes."

"But how? How can she be okay if she's being used? You're telling me she will be?" *"Yes!"* (The swinger all but flew out into a huge circle to the right, meaning "Yes, damn it all! That's what we said, and that's what we mean!")

"Have I been used by The Others?" "Yes." Oh wow! That was the first direct answer like that I had ever gotten.

"Is this crap going to stop soon?" The swinger made a

half-turn to the right, meaning, "it could, but it's not sure." Hot damn, I was on to something.

The answers didn't come overnight, because my questions weren't always the right ones. I was finding out about my guides, about my Primary Guide, about my consciousness, and about my contracts with The Light to be used by The Others as an experiment. A tit-for-tat part of Abe's deal. Whoa.

I was finding out about how millions upon this plane were now being maneuvered and used by The Others, simply because of their mix.

I was finding out how every single person on this planet was a potential catch to go through this same hell I'd been going through, which could mean anything from my own type of agony where, indeed, I was being bifurcated for use by The Others outside of this universe, or, just where parts of beings were being taken for God-knows-what.

I was finding out how the deal between Abe and his brother had been just recently broken, so now it was no-holds-barred, full-fledged, go-get-'em war from the Light.

As long as I prefaced my questions with, "In the name of the Light . . . ." I'd get direct answers. But if I were to ask the same questions without that preface, I'd get an entirely different answer. Two and two were finally making four, not five. Now all I had to do was uncover the key to getting this horror stopped. I knew it had better be soon, or this body was going to fold. My newest fear now was that my poor beleaguered body might fold before I had a chance to unlock the precious answers to questions I had been asking for years. As much as I wanted out, I wanted answers even more.

Hallelujah, a Friend

Considering that I had all but extinguished just about every friendship I'd ever had, when a new one popped up who was going through even worse than what I was going through, I leaped at her like a hungry tiger. To this day, I have never met this new friend, but to me, she was a jewel more precious than Life itself.

Bailey was, and is, a highly spiritual and highly enlightened individual. Her quest for spiritual enlightenment had been far longer than mine and much more intense, but now her agony had become excruciating to her. Even so, in the midst of such terrible pains, she would write me of her thoughts, and of her agonies, and of her determination. Bailey was becoming my emotional savior.

Along with me, Bailey had been through the "channeled teacher" routine, however she put such a different spin on the half truths she'd get from those sessions that her interpretations became an adventure—if not always a joy—for me to experience.

148

Unlike me, who saw nothing, heard nothing (except in thought), and felt nothing except excruciating, debilitating pain, Bailey seemed to see it all, and it was beyond torture. She'd see entities crawling up her legs. She'd see them going up and around and in and out of her torso. She'd feel them taking stuff out of her brain and her spinal column. She'd see little pink lights messing with her e-mails when she was trying to describe to me on the computer what was happening to her.

She knew that parts of her were being removed from her body such as her genetic coding, and parts of her brain tissue, and sections of her second brain that is housed in the solar plexus, but she didn't know why. She only knew that she was being horribly misused.

We agonized together daily via e-mail for several months. Bailey would spend hours researching Internet connections to various channeled sources, knowing that most, now, were just ca-ca, yet might hold a modicum of truth here or there. Like myself, that's all she was grabbing for: a little integrity here or there that might fit like a piece of a gigantic jigsaw puzzle into the perfect place to create—at long last—a picture of truth.

Bailey had been going through this horror for a year or so more than me. Good God, how could any human survive that kind of physical and emotional punishment? And she knew, long before I did, that The Others were having their way with her—and with us. The thought was not particularly appealing.

And there were other friends of hers who were going through it too, this ungodly nightmare of horror. It was beginning to make sense to me, but I didn't like the picture that was emerging. Not one bit. It was ugly. It was mean. It was disgusting.

How I can ever thank that woman, I'll never know, but because of her inconceivable anguish, mixed with my own, I finally broke through with my tail up over the dash to find the missing pieces. Goddamn it to holy hell, I'd find a way to stop this unconscionable incursion of the human race, no matter what I had to endure to get to that answer. Yes, I would. By God, I would!

YYY~EEEE~SSSSSS!

My swinger was acting like a little puppy just let out of its cage for the first time in its life. As long as I prefaced my questions with, "In the name of the Light . . . .," there was never a contradiction, never an inconsistency. Oh God, this was like finding Mecca, wherever that is. This was like having the answers of the universe unfold before me in all of their long-hidden glory. This was, quite frankly, heaven.

Oh sure, I was still feeling like a piece of over-broiled meat, but that was okay. All I had to do was find the right

question. Find the right question. Find the right question,
a project not quite as easy as I had hoped it would be.

Then one awful day my guides started messing with me
again, even with my preface of, "In the name of the
Light . . . " Damn! That made no sense. What was going
on?

The messing didn't stop. My answers were once again
off the wall, kooky, nuts, and in direct contradiction to
what I felt to be the truth, or to the answers I had gotten
before. Damn! DAMN! What was going on? Were my
answers-to-come just a dream? Oh please no! Were they
really?

How can you explain that moment when you "get it"?!
At that golden moment in time, you know this is it. This
is what you've been after. This is the big banana. I wish I
could tell you how these questions started with me, but I
can't. They just came.

"Do I need to change my guide team around?" *"Yes!"*
The swinger swung around like a berserk whip.

"Is that all I have to do?" *"No!"* The swinger was still
acting like a kid cut loose in a candy store.

I thought for a long time, then it was as clear as
polished crystal.

"Do I need to change my primary entity, or Primary
Guide?" The swinger all but leaped up to kiss me. "YES!"

"Is that all?" "No."

"Well, all that's left is my consciousness, and I've

already changed all that needs to be changed of that, haven't I?" "NO!!!!" Holy mackerel. I thought the thing would come up and hit me in the face.

"All right. I still need to change my consciousness mix? Shoot, I don't like to do that. No matter, is that what I need to do?" "YYY-EEEE-SSSSS!" The poor little piece of rock was flying around like it had been bitten by a bumble bee.

"Are you sure? Is that really all I have to do, aside from changing my guides and Primary Guide/entity?" *"YYY-EEEE-SSSSS!"* I got the message.

The Last Ones

By the next day I had stated all three of these intentions to clean up my "mix." I didn't care how much of the dark needed to be cleaned up, I just wanted it done. I could feel the effects of the consciousness changing setting in, sort of a minor little woozy feeling, so asked if I should go out for a walk to help integrate the new energies (I had done this before, and still have no idea why I had to do it again. No one's talking.).

Yep, start walking. I was already feeling better, so figured I could get up enough steam to walk for a little while, at least. Something about getting the heart rate going so the blood gets to the brain to help out the poor entity(s) of so much higher frequency to squeeze that little piece of itself (themselves) into a space and framework of much lower frequency. Whew!

Oh well, you get it. Walking helps. So, three times a day for half an hour each and for three days, I was either outside or on my treadmill. Walking! I could hardly believe it. *Walking!* My God, I was walking!

Every question I asked was always prefaced with "In the name of the Light . . . " In a few days I checked in to see if I was done; to see if this nightmare was really over. "Is there anything else I need to do?"

"Yes." I was furious.

"You told me it was just those three things! Damn it all, what now? Damn you, WHAT NOW!?"

My good old guides of the Light knew what they were doing, and knew me well. If they had overloaded me with these next few steps, along with the first three, they figured that in my state I'd just get confused and probably do nothing. So, they waited.

"All right, all right. Now what? And is this the last?"
"Yes."

"Promise?" "Yes."

"Okay, what now?" Thoughts were suddenly cascading over me like water from a shower. Four more simple things to do, each of which made perfect sense to me, particularly Number One which involved my dog, Lucy.

A week later, after doing all of these things, Lucy was acting like a young imp again for the first time in years. I was well on the road to recovery, and I knew this book had to be written as soon as possible.

Here are the last steps which are also nothing more than simple—but meaningful—statements:

1. **From the Light of God that I am, I call forth that all things, whether animate or inanimate, within or around me, my home, yard, or place of business, be immediately deactivated from use as "directional beacons" by those who are not of 100 percent pure Light. I further declare that when this has been accomplished, it shall be irrevocable and permanent.**

(Lucy had been being used as a directional beacon for The Others, along with some of my tapes, and who knows what else.)

2. **From the Light of God that I am, I call forth that no energies, entities, or beings are to be allowed anywhere around me at any time that are not of 100 percent pure Light. I further declare this to be irrevocable and permanent.**

(This does not always mean "bad guys." It can also mean just too many "unnecessaries" hanging around all the time, causing problems.)

3. **From the Light of God that I am, be it known that I hereby cancel all contracts and/or**

> **agreements I have made with ANY entity, in any time frame or in any reality, that were not in my best interest or in the interest of the Light, or that were made with entities who were not of 100 percent pure Light. I further declare that the cancellation of all such contracts is to be irrevocable and permanent in all time frames and realities.**

This last one is not really a step, but I'm putting it in here as one, so it will be easier to remember.

> **4. Don't ever, ever ask for guidance without demanding that what comes through be only of 100 percent pure Light, or declaring, if you're using a "swinger," the usual "in the name of the Light."**

By the way, I'm told it's best to state all of these, including those in the previous chapter, out loud. I'm told it's not really necessary . . . just a good idea. Beats me why, but hey, why not?

The days that followed were better than falling in love, better than winning the lottery, and probably the happiest days of my long life. I was actually coming out of that slimy, torturous pit I had gotten myself into.

Lucy was turning back into a dog I hardly

remembered. My mind was working, slowly at first, but I could feel the rusty wheels beginning to turn once again. After three years of unimaginable hell and three years before that of misery, dear God in heaven, I was coming out of it.

If you're in it now, you can come out of this too. If you haven't been tapped yet, once you declare these steps, you never will be. Not bad for a few minutes of meaningful concentration.

Oh man alive, *not . . . bad . . . at . . . all!!!*

chapter eight

feeding your new crew

So now you're washed, powdered, and diapered with your new, highly devoted team of entities of the Light. Good for you!

If you're still feeling a little woozy with the change of consciousness, spend as much time as possible doing some brisk walking several times a day. That woozy feeling will be gone in a day or two.

Yes, But . . .

Granted, we've been deceived about our free will while in human form. But it was necessary, in order to achieve the forthcoming birth.

Granted, we've been told that we were all children of the stars, sired by the Light. Well, that's true, but in the murk that's been created by The Others, trying to find that Light within us has often seemed this side of hopeless.

"How?"

"Where?"

"What Light? What are you talking about?"

"I've tried for years."

"I don't know anything about a spark."

"Yes, I know of my spark, but how do I find it?"

"Tell me how. Oh please, tell me how."

"Maybe another book will have the answer."

"Or another seminar. Or maybe . . . "

We search and search, but our lives remain the same. We try and try harder, but nothing happens. We go to workshops, pay for readings, pray in consecrated houses, and meditate until we're purple, but nothing happens. We know we're on the right path, but why is this path to the Light so brutally craggy, so desperately hard to follow?

Until now, none of the great masters who have come to help have been allowed to tell us, in so many words, what was going on. Oh, they've all alluded to it and talked around it. But none have told us how—or why—so much freedom within this universe was granted to The Others. None have told us how deeply each and every one of us have been affected for countless centuries by the presence of The Others.

But times have changed. That free rein for The Others

is no longer going to be allowed. The gloves are off and the guns of the Light are on lock and load. A whole bunch of us are going to be on our way to freedom, not just for the first time in centuries, but in fact, for the first time since the human species began.

Only a few hundred thousand will read this book, but the change from those thousands will dramatically affect mass consciousness. I'm told the overall change is going to be profound, but of course, not for everyone. And that's what we need to focus on now.

Let It Go, Let It Go, Let It Go

This third-dimension world we live in will continue to go through appalling situations, though not on the discouraging doomsday scale that has so often been predicted.

Nonetheless, wars will continue and in fact escalate. Earth changes will increase. Global warming will accelerate. More species of wildlife will continue to fade away (as they eagerly re-embody on the much safer Planet Two). Suicides will increase. Depression will become a planetary affliction. Events causing mass deaths will climb in number, and on and on and on. Some of this will be from the effects of Psi; more will be from The Others.

The Others will still be here, doing their thing, messing

with our emotions, screwing around with our genetic codes and whatever else they're so frantic to get, for years to come but with a reduced strength.

Regardless of that, we now have only one job to do, after doing our steps, and that is to ignore—*I-G-N-O-R-E*—whatever is happening in the rest of the world.

That's right, ignore it! Because if you don't, you'll be feeding The Others with your "ain't it awful" emotions that flood our world after every mass catastrophe.

Sound crass? You're right, it is. Thousands killed on 9/11, women being tortured and beaten in the Middle East, earthquakes killing thousands more, millions being laid off in corporate down-sizing, two thousand teens a month committing suicide, countless little ones being raped and killed or kidnapped, plagues that are wiping out whole communities (and will continue to do so); all of it, leave it alone. Let it go. LET IT GO!!!

If you need to send some sort of feeling to those in trouble, send only—and I do mean ONLY—this to those in need or who are left behind:

It's going to be all right.
You're going to be all right.
Everything's going to be all right.

Send that with love, not with sorrow or melancholy, and you won't be feeding The Others.

Instead, you'll be overriding the effects of Psi, and you'll be feeding your new crew of Light, rather than sapping their strength, which happens every time you immerse yourself in the "ain't it awful" syndrome. Plus, you'll be sending a helping hand to those affected, rather than encircling them in a frequency of gloom, which is so prevailing in major disasters.

Let it go. Leave it alone. Let it all go. If you can't send a warm blanket of, "It's going to be all right," don't send a thing.

Habits Be Gone

If you've read *Excuse Me, Your Life is Waiting*, some of this may seem redundant. Ah yes, but refreshers and reminders never hurt any of us, right?

And if you have read *Excuse Me . . .* and have had a hard time keeping the techniques going, join the group. So many of the e-mails I get tell me how wonderful they thought the book was, how it filled in all the long years of searching, how they enthusiastically put the principles to use, and then . . . "but how do I keep it going? How do I keep up the enthusiasm?"

Most of the time I've wanted to send back my answer with something like, "Well, Honey, when you find out, let me know!" It has not been easy to keep the more desirable feelings going, and in many cases not even possible because we've had so much interference from The Others. But now we've got some clout, and by God, let's use it!

We now have a team comprised of entities of 100 percent pure Light (or you will have, not long after doing the steps).

Imagine! We have a team who will work FOR us, rather than against us. We have a team who will do all they can within their complex parameters of your game plan, your desires, AND, your feelings and emotions, to bring some major joy into your life, some major happiness, some major fun. Your team is now dedicated to that end. But you gotta help 'em.

Habits of any kind are not easy to break. They become part of our way of life, part of our day-to-day thinking, and reactions. Habits, up to now, have defined us in our rolls as Fathers, Mothers, Siblings, Workers, Relatives, Voters, Friends, and Children of any age.

Sadly, the majority of our habits have come deliberately and with much cunning from our crappy mix of guidance and consciousness. But not just from this lifetime. The truth is that changing our mix to troops of all Light is not—repeat, NOT—going to magically wipe away habits, or customs, that have been embedded in us not only from this lifetime, but from our physical and spiritual (cosmic) genetic codings from ages past.

Don't sigh in defeat; this is changeable. It truly is, though it *will* take a bit of attention.

Feeding Our Guys

We need to find ways to generate positive emotions, as often as we can. Period. If you haven't read *Excuse Me, Your Life is Waiting*, then I'd strongly suggest you get it, for everything in there is not only a hallowed truth, but is now more important than ever.

Yes, we are generators of waves of energy that carry with them a particular vibratory frequency based on what emotion we were feeling at the time we sent that wave out.

Yes, we have been generating waves of low-frequency negativity most of our lives. Some of that has been because of our mix. Some of that has been because of the massive negative energies in which we live that have been generated by everyone else's mix. And some, more recently, has been from Psi.

Granted, we haven't known about this frequency business until recently, but whether we've just recently gotten the information or are getting it now, the point is we've got to pay attention to what we're flowing out of us. We need to feed our new team all the high frequency vibes we can. That, in and of itself, is really no big deal. But it most assuredly is necessary.

So how do we do this up-the-frequency thing? How do we flip from the habit of "damn you" that vibrationally feeds The Others, to the new habit of a different kind of feeling, and mean it? How do we flip from the chronic habit of worry that feeds The Others, to something else?

Remember, anything below middle C is in the negative column of vibrational frequency, no matter how slight, and is food for The Others and bad news for you. Anything that even remotely causes you to feel just a little better than what you felt a moment ago will be above middle C, providing food for your new team, and far better circumstances and happenings for you.

All right. I hate sounding so ironhanded, but the truth is, if we don't do these things at least some of the time during the day to patch the wounds of ages past, it's going to be awfully hard for "our guys" to do their things to help us into our new beginnings. And believe me, they want to help you with every loving piece of Light that is within them.

Flip Switching!

No one, for as long as we're on this planet, is going to flow yum-yum positive energy all day long. Yet that's what all the positive thinking books suggest we should do. "Find your joy." Lovely, but did anyone ever tell us how? Or, for that matter, why? Not in my lifetime.

"When you are in joy, you are in alignment with the universe." How nice.

"Joy is the magic genie of life." Swell. So who has the roadmap?

The only roadmap there will ever be, for as long as we're in this reality, is learning how to briefly Flip Switch rather than trying to achieve some impossibly lofty goal of staying happy all the time. Good luck. It'll never happen. But now, with our mix of 100 percent pure Light, Flip Switching won't be nearly as hard.

First of all, remember that what we think equals what we feel, and what we feel equals how we vibrate, and how we vibrate equals how we attract. With that in mind, what then is Flip Switching?

Flip Switching is simply an action you take yourself to get from a low vibration to a higher one. It's your insistence on finding a way to change (flip)—IN THE MOMENT—using your imagination.

That means learning to flip—right now!—out of the habit of even mild negativity (when you become aware of it) to a vibration that makes you feel even a little bit better. In the now. In the moment. Straightaway! Right off the bat!

And for Pete's sake, we're not talking extremes here. We're not talking hate, or malice, or resentment, or utter hopelessness (which would all be WAY below middle C).

And we're not talking euphoria, or ecstasy, or being in so-called nirvana (all of which would be way above middle C).

No. We're just talking a key or two below or above the middle, which is where most of us live most of our lives.

It's those vibrations above the middle that will turn the corner for us, feed our new crew, and bring us much more of what we're looking for in life.

Flip Switching is about:

- looking for ways to feel better in any one given moment, no matter what is happening around you

- finding ways to feel better, when everything is going well

- finding ways to feel better when you don't want to

- finding ways to feel better when your Want seems nowhere in sight

- finding ways to feel better when those around you may be in a mess

- finding ways to feel better when you feel like everything is against you

- finding ways to feel better when you know, you absolutely know, it's all lost, done, finished for you

- finding ways to feel better when you feel good, or okay, or great, or fine, and everything is going right

Flip Switching is NOT about:

- getting others to act the way you'd like them to act

- trying to *feeeeel* your desire to save someone, if their intent (either consciously or unconsciously) is to leave this reality

- finding a better mate, or house, or car, if you haven't decided yet to vibrationally override what your present feelings are about the one you want to leave behind

- using your past as an excuse for whatever kind of feelings or mess you're into now (excuses vibrate WAY below middle C)

- trying to get rich quick

- trying to "fix" things for your own presumed benefit

- wanting everything to happen now

- trying to fix things for others

- thinking you have to stay in la-la happy-land all day long (trust me, that will never happen)

In the Moment

Flip Switching is an activity—in the moment—that you

engage in for the benefit of yourself, and ONLY yourself. Others may or may not benefit from your efforts, but that is not your role in life. Your role is to "get it," meaning to learn what your enormous, untapped clout really is, now that you've freed yourself from the vicious constraints of The Others. The Psi energies will still be with you, but you'll be okay.

Flip Switching is NOT about making instant miracles, or instant riches, or instant anything. If you have fast results, fantastic. But remember, we're talking entrenched habits of not only this lifetime, but from countless lifetimes past. Addiction to pain—emotional pain—is mankind's single most disastrous habit. Meaning, this is just going to take a little effort, a little work, a bit of attention everyday. Not all day, but every day. So let's go.

Here are just a few ways to Flip Switch in the moment. And remember, it's always in the moment, because all you need are a few seconds here, a few seconds there, then a few more here and there as this becomes easier and easier for you.

Feeeeel what it's like to cuddle a new little puppy (or a kitten, if you don't dig dogs). Those are above-middle-C vibrations flowing from you, just what we're looking for. Okay, now flow out that same *feeeeeling,* just for a few seconds, to:

- the pencil on your desk

- your door knob

- every red light you see

- the speck of dust on your dresser

- your toothbrush

- your computer

- your dork of a boss

- your empty checkbook (no fair thinking about money)

- your bathroom towel (when no one's watching, go ahead and caress it)

- the nitwit on the freeway

- every green car on the road

- every bug you see

All right, enough. You get the idea. The point is to find ways every day, no matter how you may feel in the moment, to flow out some Feel-Better vibrations.

You do this, even for a few seconds, when you feel lousy, or mad, or sad.

You do this, even for a few seconds, when you feel terrific.

You do this as many times during the day as you possibly can remember to do it. Because every time you do this for even ten seconds, you are overriding around a year of negative flow. Not too shabby.

If you can build up, cumulatively (not all at once) to a total of ten minutes a day, you'll start to see so many wonderful things happen in your life; it will make your head spin. All that's required is a few seconds every day of flipping from normal "down," to not-normal warm fuzzies, any way you can.

A Few More Ideas

Now here's how to feel like a real nut-case, while getting those inner frequencies up at the same time. Remember, raising our frequencies *naturally* is what we're after. It's the abnormal forcing of our frequencies that we've been getting, both personally and world-wide, that has pushed so many challenging buttons in us. Back to feeling like a nut-case.

SING your shopping list! SING (as quietly as you want) to your body. HUM in the shower. HUM as you vacuum, or as you get on the subway, or change the beds, or head for the board meeting. Hum, sing, make the noise that creates—and then flows—the higher inner vibration. That's just as effective as flowing appreciation to your doorknob. A few seconds here, a few seconds, there will give your new team the vibrations they need, and get you out of the habit of either flat-lining (feeling nothing), or being in a constant downer.

The other easy thing to do—when no one's looking—is to smile. Huh? That's right smile, but from the inside, not just a phony grin. *Feeeeel* what it would be like to have a toddler come up to you with a precious something to show off. You can't help getting that smile on your face that comes from deep within you. So, just create that same *feeeeeling*, and presto! You've gone to a real Feel Better, from middle or below middle C, up to a key or two or three higher. You've eradicated a year or more of negative flow in just those few seconds. And, you've fed your new team the stuff they need to help you go where you want to go. Not bad for a few seconds of concentration.

The whole idea is to create a new habit. Just because you've chased away those turkeys we call The Others from your life doesn't mean the tooth fairy is going to deposit instant happiness into your lap. You're going to have to take some responsibility, and give your new team a helping hand.

If your habit has always been (as it was mine) one of momentary impatience when the waitress didn't bring your food on time, or your mate didn't do something-or-other as promised or as scheduled, or the service man didn't come when he was supposed to, that's when you Flip Switch.

If something hasn't happened the way you want it to happen, then Flip Switch to any kind of a Feel Better as often as you can. You don't have to think about anything, like about the promotion you didn't get, or the love who has left you, or the humdrum of your life. Just Flip Switch as often as you can, find ways for just a few seconds to promote a Feel Better, and I promise you, magic will happen.

Flip Switch in every moment you think about it, no matter how you feel. Flip Switch when you're feeling down, and Flip Switch when you're feeling up.

Put on that inner smile and see how long you can keep it going.

Hum a tune, anytime, anywhere, for as long as you can.

Flow warm fuzzies of appreciation toward anything, and keep it flowing for longer this time.

There's nothing woo-woo about this. It's pure physics. Like frequencies attract like frequencies, meaning what you flow out from the inside will find its match, and magnetically bring something back to you to correspond to the feeling you flowed out. Plus . . . this will feed your wonderfully loving new team. That's all there is to Flip Switching, just finding ways now and then to feel better. That's really all there is to it.

Oh, and for Psi? If you can find 15 minutes in every day to get some sunshine (even from sunshine parlors), that will help produce more necessary serotonin in your brain. There are also natural substances you can take to produce more of this neurotransmitter, but that should be up to your doctor or health practitioner.

Coming Off of Rote

For this whole thing to work, life can no longer be mechanical or routine for any of us. We're going to have to put some effort into it, or we'll quickly fall back into the cavern of negative social consciousness with which we're all surrounded, whether we've changed our mix or not.

When disasters happen, either flow "it's going to be all right" to the victims, or Flip Switch, however is easiest for you, or let it go.

When messes are happening around you, Flip Switch.

When you're feeling fine and dandy, Flip Switch.

In other words, get out of the habit of staying in what appears to be a normal vibration, and get into the habit of creating a new one. That's all there is to it.

But oh, how important!

And Finally . . .

We've been told over and over that the power to create our lives the way we want them to be has always been within us. We've been told this until we don't want to hear it any more. We been told that we create our own reality. Well, if that's so true, why hasn't it happened? Now, I hope, we know.

It hasn't happened because we had The Others working against us.

It hasn't happened because now we even have the Light, with Psi, working somewhat against us, and yet for us.

We've found it difficult to remain out of fear and despair because we've had The Others working against us.

Flowing positive energy has been fine, for a while, but then we've found ourselves falling back into that same old rut of mild, moderate, or even heavy negativity, because we've had The Others working against us.

So don't hold yourself at fault, and for sure don't hold anyone else at fault either. This is a new time, a new awareness unprecedented in the annals of mankind.

We know now what has been happening to us, and we know the actions that we, at least, can take. Maybe those actions from all of us will only mildly change the world's negativity. But one thing is for certain: it will change ours.

As you implement these steps, maybe with trepidation and uncertainty, maybe with doubt, maybe with hesitation, I ask that you remember that you are, indeed, a child of the stars, sired by the Light.

I ask that you remember that you never again have to dream those dreams of dread or terror.

I ask you to remember that, in doing what you will do or have done with these steps, you have changed not only your own life, but the fate of mankind in a manner never accomplished before, for eons past.

And finally, I ask you to remember how truly loved you are, and how deeply you are honored for the actions you are taking, or have taken, or will soon be taking to sweep away the influence of The Others from yourself and from your surroundings.

I'm told that for you and for each of us who do this, the impact will be felt throughout all of the universe, throughout all of the Isness, for all of eternity.

So go for it.

epilogue

Oh man. Everything in me doesn't want to write these next lines, but I know I have to. To put this into print may seem as if everything you've just read is a lie, and that this is just a copout to cover my tail. It is not. Oh please, I promise you that it is not.

There are approximately one hundred people on this planet, from all over the world, who will be doing something for the Light that may feel similar to the things I've described. But they will not be similar, and they will not be anywhere near to what I've described.

Those one hundred people signed on to help create a new grid of Light for this planet to help out now, before the birth, and to assist in every possible way after the birth. But honestly, it will be nothing like what I've gone through. Here's how it will probably come down for them:

Once the energies begin with someone, they may last— off and on—for two to three years. But, these folks will experience discomfort for only a day at a time (!!!!!)—perhaps two or three times a week. Sometimes those energies will be unpleasant, other times they'll be not so bad, but it will never, ever be continuous, day after day as it was with me.

This group is, well, somewhat unique, because they signed up before coming in here to help out in a way they knew was going to be disagreeable. You may be one.

I have a friend who was in this group, and the worst she experienced were a few days in bed that were difficult, a few days out back screaming to the universe to get it stopped since she had no idea what was happening, and then several days of just going through it.

That lasted with her for about two years, off and on, mostly off.

You just need to know it's a possibility, but for heaven's sake, that doesn't mean you should ignore the steps in this book. Not at all. . . . Not at all!

What's happening with this group is that they are acting as conduits for the incoming Psi energies, and then downloading those energies into grid sections, all around the earth. I'd love to know what I'm talking about, but that's about all I can offer.

If, in a week or two after doing your thing with these steps, you find yourself feeling unpleasant energies, you may be one of these special few. Not to worry, it will never get to be horribly unpleasant for very long. Just know you've signed on to do an extraordinary thing.

If You Teach . . . Or . . .

Seminars, workshops, study groups, speaking engagements, newsletters, counseling, writing books, hosting talk shows, chatting with friends and family . . .

The steps in this book need to get out there to as wide an audience as we can find, just as soon as possible. If you talk at times with a lot of people, or a small group, or just one on one, for each individual you talk with who sincerely implements these steps, a powerful change within this reality will take place, and always, *always* with the domino effect. A change in one will affect many. So you see the immense potential.

Take whatever you want from the book (yes please, with appropriate credit to title, author, and publisher), and use as much of it as you will in seminars or workshops or any place else.

If folks want to buy the book, great! Hampton Roads Publishing and I will thank you, but that's not necessary to get this vital information disseminated. This book is merely the kindling. Fanning the crucial fire is up to you.

Please, No Questions!

For the last few years I've been receiving letters and e-mails from folks who have read my other books, and from experience, I know that people turn to authors for every kind of advice imaginable. Although I have answered these letters (and now just e-mails) in general, they have rarely been with a definitive answer, as I'm not licensed to do that.

My job, as an author, is to impart information. I am not a therapist, I am not a counselor, and I most surely am not in any way a medical advisor.

If you e-mail me with medical questions, or if you want to know what's happening to you because of such and such symptoms, or whether you should go see a doctor, or about anything that has to do with your health or well-being, I WILL NOT ANSWER.

In fact, I'll be answering no questions at all. If you want to respond via e-mail regarding how this has helped you, or how *Excuse Me* . . . has helped you, or the *Playbook* or whatever, I'll respond as time permits. Visit www.lynngrabhorn.com for details. But please, no questions about how to run your life, or what to do with your lover, or if "these symptoms" that you may have are what I'm talking about in this book. Okay?

We're all in for a helluva ride right now, so let's just fasten our seat belts, execute the steps, thumb our noses at what may have been pulling us down, and have a ball with the rest of our lives: now, and forevermore.

Many thanks!
Lynn Grabhorn

About the Author

Lynn Grabhorn is a long-time student of the way in which thought and feelings format our lives. Raised in Short Hills, New Jersey, she began her working life in the advertising field in New York City, founded and ran an audio-visual educational publishing company in Los Angeles, and owned and ran a mortgage brokerage firm in Washington State.

Lynn's books, *Excuse Me, Your Life Is Waiting*, *The Excuse Me, Your Life Is Waiting Playbook*, and *Beyond the Twelve Steps*, along with her sweeping multimedia program, *Life Course 101*, have received high acclaim from all corners of the world. She lives near Olympia, where she continues to write and "mow my five acres."

Hampton Roads Publishing Company

. . . for the evolving human spirit

Hampton Roads Publishing Company
publishes books on a variety of subjects including
metaphysics, health, visionary fiction,
and other related topics.

For a copy of our latest catalog,
call toll-free, 800-766-8009,
or send your name and address to:

Hampton Roads Publishing Company, Inc.
1125 Stoney Ridge Road
Charlottesville, VA 22902
e-mail: hrpc@hrpub.com
www.hrpub.com